PUBLISHER:
SPORTS GRAPHICS INTERNATIONAL
PRODUCTS, INC.
7100 FRANCE AVENUE SOUTH
EDINA, MINNESOTA 55435

© COPYRIGHT 1980 BY CAROLYN REICHOW
AND DOROTHIE A. DEKKO

ISBN: 0-960 4214-0-8

COMPILED AND WRITTEN BY
RUTH ARNOLD-KENEFICK
CAROLYN REICHOW
AND DOTTIE DEKKO
RECIPES TESTED BY:
DOTTIE DEKKO, HOME ECONOMIST
ART DIRECTION AND DESIGN:
JEFF FARMAKES

A STANDING OVATION TO JERRY REICHOW —
our M.V.P. Thanks for your clout, your special trivia
knowledge and your advice. Without your All-Pro
patience, we wouldn't have this book.

A special thanks to Nancy Stidger, Leslie West,
Barb Faber and Grace Stidger as a great "back up
team." A warm thank-you to all of our patient
testers — your help and time was greatly
appreciated.

N F L

COOKBOOK

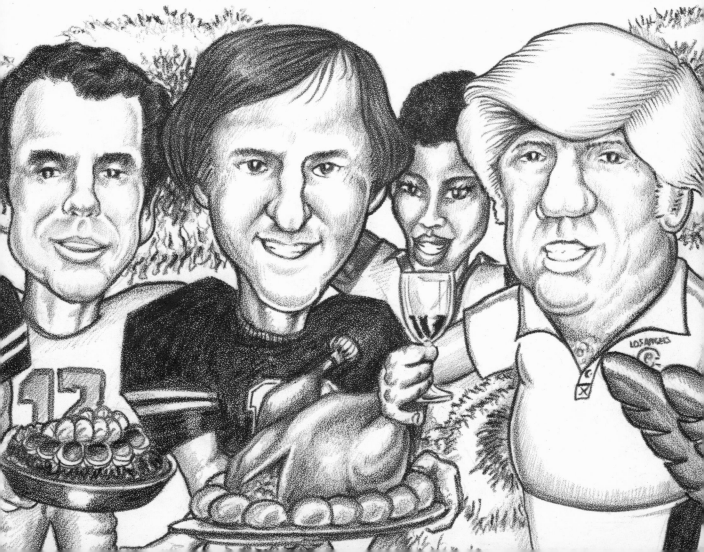

COMMENTARY FROM THE FRONT OFFICE

Dear Readers, Food Lovers, Professional Tailgaters, Football Fans, Cooking Enthusiasts, Non-Enthusiastic Cooks and the rest of America (doesn't that about sum it up?),

Welcome to the wonderful world of eating and football excitement. Please read on to the letter Sports Graphics sent out to the celebrated individuals in football and you'll understand the whys and why nots of this cookbook. Then go on to test, taste, sample, sip, nibble, gobble and enjoy the recipes — explained play by play — from famous football personalities and then some.

Yours in good eating,
The Editors

Greetings from Sports Graphics,

Americans love football, its fine players and personalities, past and present. You are an outstanding member of this group. Everyone agrees this group has produced some of the finest "National Food Lovers" in the country — resulting in the title and concept of Sports Graphics' new cookbook — "National Food Lovers." The book will promote and stir up lots of excitement for the game, the fun and the food.

We intend to keep the cookbook casual — nothing too fancy or complicated — just good eating. We would love recipes from you that are the favorites in your life or family — for example; childhood favorites, Grandma's prize, Grandpa's boast, Mom's creation, Dad's secret, your wife's best, a neighbor's surprise, or whomever your favorite cook may be. Above all, if *you* are your favorite cook, so much the better!

We are curious to hear your comments about the recipe. We will include them as "Notes from the Bench" along with your recipe to add personal spice and flair. We ask three recipes from you for testing purposes and to avoid any possible duplication. We'll publish everything from appetizers to desserts.

We look forward to your contributions and to having you join other nationally recognized food lovers of the N.F.L.

Most sincerely,

Carolyn Reichou   *Ruth Arnold-Kenefick*

Sports Graphics International Products

Lottie Stekko

THE PLAY BOOK

CHALK TALK

In the football spirit, we've re-titled most of the recipes — how many of your Triscuits have tackled a "First String Salmon Mousse" or how many of you can proudly say you've served a "Suicide Squad Garlic Pizza"? Well, they're all here.

The "Notes from the Bench" are exactly that. They're our contributors' personal comments and suggestions along with their signatures. The "Referee's Notes", of course, are editorial comments — just to keep the game going.

To avoid too much time in the huddle, the "Game Plan" section diagrams some spectacular menus.

Too many times when getting ready for that special meal, it isn't the cooking, it's the decisions. We've offered a few sure-fire menus for you to try.

Our "National Food Lovers Hall of Fame" section gives a brief football history of each of our featured "players." Enjoy and learn.

The trivia — that's for you to figure out! Throughout, there are memory joggers for all who claim to be whiz kids at little-known football facts. Good luck with them.

Now, let's get out there and win this one for the cook!

THE PRE-GAME WARM UP

BART'S FAVORITE CUCUMBER DIP

1 - 8 OZ. PKG. PHILADELPHIA CREAM CHEESE

½ CUCUMBER, UNPEELED

2 TBSP. MAYONNAISE

GARLIC SALT

SPRINKLE OF DILL

by CHERRY STARR

(Bart Starr, General Manager, Head Coach, Green Bay Packers)

Grate cucumber, pour off extra juice and use later for proper consistency. Beat cheese, mayonnaise until smooth. Add cucumber, salt and dill. Blend. Add extra juice if too thick. Use as a dip with chips or crackers or as an open-faced party sandwich with a slice of cucumber and sprig of parsley.

NOTES FROM THE BENCH: *"This is Bart's favorite dip. He eats it almost every night. It's so fattening, so I sit and watch!"*

Cherry Starr

SEAHAWK'S SMOKY SALMON SPREAD

1 - 7¾ OZ. CAN SALMON OR ½ LB. SMOKED SALMON

1 - 8 OZ. PKG. SOFTENED CREAM CHEESE

1 TBSP. LEMON JUICE

2 TSP. ONION, GRATED

2 TSP. HORSERADISH

¼ TSP. LIQUID SMOKE (IF CANNED SALMON)

SALT AND PEPPER TO TASTE

¼ C. PECANS, CHOPPED

2 TBSP. PARSLEY, CHOPPED

by JOHN THOMPSON

(General Manager, Seattle Seahawks)

Drain and flake salmon. Combine with cream cheese, lemon juice, onion, horseradish, liquid smoke, salt and pepper. Blend thoroughly. Shape mixture into a ball on waxed paper. Wrap and chill for several hours. Combine pecans and parsley on waxed paper. Roll salmon spread ball in pecans and parsley to coat. Chill. Makes 2½ cups.

REFEREE'S NOTE: *Leave it to the Seahawks to concoct such a delicious salmon appetizer!*

"KICKOFF" MUSHROOMS

1 LB. FRESH MUSHROOMS

¾ C. OIL

⅓ C. WINE VINEGAR

3 TSP. CHIVES, CHOPPED OR ONIONS

1 TSP. TARRAGON

1 CLOVE GARLIC, MINCED

½ TSP. SUGAR

2 BAY LEAVES, CRUSHED

by RICH SAUL

(#61, C, Los Angeles Rams)

Boil everything but mushrooms for 5 mins. Cool. Add mushrooms and marinate 12 hours or more. Serve with toothpicks. Serves 10-12.

NOTES FROM THE BENCH: *"A good way to whet your appetite."*

Rich Saul

"FIRST STRING" SALMON MOUSSE

2 CANS, 1 LB. SIZE, RED SALMON
½ C. CIDER VINEGAR
½ C. SOUR CREAM
2 TBSP. HORSERADISH
2 ENVELOPES UNFLAVORED GELATIN
½ C. LEMON JUICE
1 TSP. SEASONED SALT
1 TBSP. PREPARED MUSTARD
1 C. HEAVY CREAM, WHIPPED

by MAXINE FINKS
(Jim Finks, General Manager, Chicago Bears)

Drain salmon, remove bones and skin. Break into small pieces. In electric blender, blend salmon and vinegar to make puree. Turn in large bowl and fold in sour cream and horseradish. In measuring cup, sprinkle gelatin over lemon juice — let stand 5 mins. Set in pan of boiling water. Stir to dissolve. Stir into salmon mixture with salt and mustard. Fold into whipped cream — turn into a 1½ qt. mold. Refrigerate covered until firm — 4 hours. Serves about 12.

REFEREE'S NOTE: There's nothing like a Bear's mousse.

Q. What former pro was the 1955 Heisman Trophy winner? Hint: Ohio State. *Answer page 105.*

"WING-T" CHICKEN WINGS

4 LBS. CHICKEN WINGS, SPLIT
1 JAR APRICOT PRESERVES
1 BOTTLE OF WISHBONE RUSSIAN SALAD DRESSING
1 ENVELOPE LIPTON ONION SOUP

by PETER CRONAN
(#57, LB, Seattle Seahawks)

Mix preserves, dressing and soup together. Pour over chicken and marinate overnight. Bake at 350° for ½ hour until chicken is brown. Stir often. Serves 10-12.

NOTES FROM THE BENCH: "Make sure you have plenty of napkins, 'finger lickin' good.'"

RON'S "WARM UP" CHILI DIP

1 CAN HORMEL CHILI (WITHOUT BEANS)
1 SMALL JAR CHEEZ WHIZ
1 CAN O&C FRENCH FRIED ONIONS
TABASCO OR HOT PEPPERS TO TASTE

by RON ERHARDT
(Head Coach, New England Patriots)

Heat and blend chili and Cheezwhiz in double boiler, add onions and hot seasonings and mix. Serve in chafing dish with plain taco chips for dipping.

NOTES FROM THE BENCH: "This dip always draws great comments. Men especially like this!"

Ronald Erhardt

A.F.C. ONION CHEESE APPETIZERS

1 C. MAYONNAISE
½ C. CHEDDAR CHEESE, GRATED
½ C. GREEN ONIONS, CHOPPED
¼ C. PARMESAN CHEESE, GRATED

by JACK KEMP
(Former Buffalo Bills QB)

Mix ingredients. Spread on Triscuits. Broil till lightly browned. Serves 10.

NOTES FROM THE BENCH: *"We eat this almost weekly while watching football games on television."*

REFEREE'S NOTES: *A superb excuse for a "delay of game."*

"CHAMPION" CRAB MEAT APPETIZERS

1 - 6½ OZ. CAN CRAB MEAT
¼ C. COLD WATER
1½ TSP. UNFLAVORED GELATIN
3 TBSP. CATSUP
2 TBSP. LOW-CALORIE FRENCH DRESSING
½ TSP. WORCESTERSHIRE SAUCE
½ TSP. SALT
¼ TSP. PAPRIKA

by DENNIS LICK
(#70, OT, Chicago Bears)

Drain crab meat — set aside. Pour water into a small cup, sprinkle unflavored gelatin evenly over water, let stand 5 mins. to soften, dissolve gelatin completely by placing cup over very hot water. Meanwhile, mix together last 5 ingredients. When gelatin is dissolved, stir and blend into catsup mixture. Add crab meat and blend. Spoon into baking cups. Freeze until firm, about 3 hours. Before serving, remove paper cups. Allow to stand a few mins. at room temperature to slightly soften. Serve on lettuce cups. 49 calories per serving. Serves 6.

REFEREE'S NOTE: *A low calorie snack to control the "spread formation."*

VIKINGS' SMOKED FISH APPETIZER

1 LB. SMOKED FISH (TROUT, SALMON OR WHITEFISH)
⅓ C. MAYONNAISE
3 TBSP. GREEN OR SPANISH ONIONS, CHOPPED

by JERRY REICHOW
(Coordinator of Football Operations, Minnesota Vikings)

Flake fish and blend all ingredients together. Serve with crackers. Great for tailgating or any kind of entertaining. Serves 8-10.

NOTES FROM THE BENCH: *"Because I'm a fisherman, this is a great way to enjoy my catch. We have our own smoker, but smoked fish are available at most supermarkets."*

MAUI MEATBALLS

1 LB. GROUND BEEF
¼ C. COCONUT, SHREDDED
⅓ C. CHUTNEY, CHOPPED
½ TSP. GARLIC SALT

by JACK CHRISTIANSEN
(Hall of Fame, Detroit Lions DB)

Mix and make into meatballs. Bake at 350° until done.

REFEREE'S NOTE: Add one egg for better consistency.

BABA GHAUNOOJ

1 MED. SIZE EGGPLANT
1 LG. GARLIC CLOVE, FINELY CHOPPED
2 TBSP. TARATOOR SAUCE
(RECIPE TO FOLLOW)
¼ C. FRESH LEMON JUICE
1 TSP. SALT
1 TBSP. OLIVE OIL
¼ C. ONION, FINELY CHOPPED
1 TBSP. PARSLEY, FINELY CHOPPED

NOTES FROM THE BENCH: "This is good served with small pieces of pocket or pita bread."

by ABE GIBRON
(Assistant Head Coach, Tampa Bay Buccaneers)

Roast egg plant (pricked in 3 or 4 places) in a slow oven until soft and the skin starts to crack. Cool. Peel and mash to smooth puree. Beat in lemon juice, Taratoor sauce, garlic and salt. Spread in serving plate and sprinkle the top with oil, onion and parsley.

TARATOOR SAUCE: 3 garlic cloves, finely chopped; 1 C. tahina paste (this can be bought in a gourmet shop); ¾ to 1 C. cold water; ½ C. fresh lemon juice; 1 tsp. salt. In deep bowl mash garlic to paste. Stir in the tahina, with a whisk beat in ½ C. cold water, lemon juice and salt. Still beating, add up to ½ C. more water, 1 Tbsp. at a time, while the sauce has the consistency of thick mayonnaise and holds its shape almost solidly in a spoon. This sauce is also very good served over baked fish or fried cauliflower.

REFEREE'S NOTE: Abe is known throughout the league as a connoisseur of fine food and wine. His Middle-Eastern heritage is evident in this recipe. Abe really scores as a true National Food Lover.

"ROOKIE" CRESCENT SQUARES

1 LB. GROUND BEEF
¼ C. ONION, CHOPPED OR
1 TBSP. MINCED ONION
1 TSP. SALT
⅛ TSP. PEPPER
2½ OZ. JAR MUSHROOMS
½ C. SOUR CREAM
8 OZ. CRESCENT ROLLS
6 SLICES AMERICAN CHEESE

by MARK KONCAR
(#79, OT, Green Bay Packers)

Spread rolls on ungreased pan; brown meat, onions, salt and pepper. Drain. Stir in mushrooms and sour cream. Spread over rolls and top with cheese. Bake at 375° for 20-25 mins.

NOTES FROM THE BENCH: "This is nice for a party appetizer or watching football games! It's tasty and a snap to make."

#182 — CRAB AND CREAM CHEESE COCKTAIL

1 - 8 OZ. PKG. CREAM CHEESE

1 LB. CRAB MEAT, CHOPPED OR SHREDDED, OR FROZEN SNOW CRAB, THAWED

1 BOTTLE SEAFOOD COCKTAIL SAUCE

VARIETY OF CRACKERS

by PAT MINER

(Tom Miner, Scout, Cleveland Browns)

Place block of cheese on plate, cover with crab meat and top with cocktail sauce. Let guests spread their own.

NOTES FROM THE BENCH: "*Since San Diego has such fantastic weather, especially during football season, Charger fans are very 'big' on tailgate parties, both before and after the games. This year for the first time, special reserve parking spaces for the season were set aside for motorhomes. This recipe was voted the favorite of Chargers fans partying each week in Space 182.*"

Pat Miner

CURRY DIP

1 C. MAYONNAISE

1 TSP. TARRAGON VINEGAR

1 TSP. CREAM-STYLE HORSERADISH

1 TSP. MINCED ONION

1 TSP. CURRY POWDER

1 TSP. GARLIC SALT

Blend well. Serve with celery and carrot sticks, cauliflower buds and zucchini squash slices.

REFEREE'S NOTE: Tastes like a million, simple to prepare ahead, no last minute fuss.

Q. The modern day Tight End was patterned after what former pro player? *Answer page 105.*

EXPERIENCED TAILGATERS' HOT CRAB MEAT DIP

2 - 10 OZ. PKGS. CREAM CHEESE

SALT TO TASTE

ONION JUICE TO TASTE

1½ TSP. FRENCH'S MUSTARD

2 CANS CRAB MEAT OR FROZEN CRAB

⅓ C. MAYONNAISE

GARLIC SALT TO TASTE

SOY SAUCE TO TASTE

3 TBSP. SAUTERNE WINE

Mix together in large kettle and heat until well blended. Put on bread rounds and broil.

REFEREE'S NOTE: Mastered at a post-game tailgate marathon in New England.

DILL DIP

1 C. MAYONNAISE

1 C. DAIRY SOUR CREAM

2 TBSP. DRIED DILL WEED

2 TBSP. DRIED PARSLEY FLAKES

2 TSP. DRIED ONION FLAKES

½ TSP. SEASONED SALT OR BEAU MONDE SEASONING

Mix well. Serve with crackers, potato chips or crisp, fresh vegetables.

REFEREE'S NOTE: *Bring this to brunch to munch with your pre-game bunch!*

Q. Who is considered by many as the greatest quarterback of all times? Hint: Played in the old All-American Football Conference. *Answer page 105.*

THE FIELD GENERAL'S ARTICHOKE ROUNDS

1 TALL CAN WHOLE ARTICHOKES

1 PKG. GARLIC OR ONION ROUNDS, BUTTERED

1 C. PARMESAN CHEESE, GRATED

¾ C. MAYONNAISE

by TOMMY KRAMER
(#9, QB, Minnesota Vikings)

Drain artichokes and cut in quarters. Spread the crackers lightly with butter. Mix cheese with mayonnaise. Place a piece of artichoke on each round of cracker and spoon enough of cheese mixture on top to cover artichoke. Bake at 375° 10 mins. or until golden in color. Watch carefully.

REFEREE'S NOTE: *Take this hot tip from Kramer for good tasting.*

Tommy Kramer

"UNDER THE DOME" APPETIZER BALL

1 LB. LIVER SAUSAGE

¼ C. MAYONNAISE

2 TBSP. DILL PICKLE JUICE

1 TSP. WORCESTERSHIRE

3 DROPS TABASCO

¼ TSP. GARLIC SALT

1 - 8 OZ. PKG. CREAM CHEESE, SOFTENED

⅓ C. CHOPPED DILL PICKLE

¼ C. ONION, FINELY CHOPPED (OPTIONAL)

½ C. SALTED PEANUTS, CHOPPED

Mash liver sausage with fork. Blend with mayonnaise, pickle juice, Worcestershire, Tabasco, garlic salt and one third the cream cheese until smooth. Stir in pickle and onion. Pack firmly into a 2-cup mixing bowl lined with saran or aluminum foil. Chill several hours, or until firm. Turn out and frost with remaining cream cheese. Chill well. Before serving, cover with peanuts. Serve with assorted crackers. Serves appetizers for 16-20.

CRAB FONDUE

½ LB. AMERICAN CHEESE

¼ LB. MARGARINE

1 CAN CRAB, DRAINED

¼ C. SHERRY

Melt cheese and margarine together. Add crab and Sherry. Serve in fondue pot with Triscuits.

REFEREE'S NOTE: Festive fondue. Try it at a tailgate.

DELUXE TAILGATE CHEESE BALL

2 - 5 OZ. JARS KRAFT SHARP OLD ENGLISH CHEESE

2 - 5 OZ. JARS KRAFT ROKA CHEESE

1 - 8 OZ. PKG. PHILADELPHIA CREAM CHEESE

8-10 OZ. IMPORTED ROQUEFORT CHEESE

2 TBSP. ONION JUICE

1½ TSP. BEAU MONDE SEASONING

½ C. PECANS, FINELY CHOPPED

½ C. PARSLEY FLAKES

VARIETY OF CRACKERS

Combine cheeses, onion juice, Beau Monde, and bring to room temperature. Blend thoroughly. Refrigerate for several hours or overnight. Form into ball. Combine pecans and parsley. On waxed paper, spread pecan mixture and roll cheese ball in mixture to coat. Serve with a variety of crackers.

REFEREE'S NOTE: One devoted tailgater admitted he would rather be awarded this cheese ball than the game ball!

Q. What current head coach played both pro football and pro basketball? *Answer page 105.*

GRANDMA'S BACON ROLL-UPS

1 CAN MUSHROOM SOUP

1 LOAF THIN SLICED SANDWICH BREAD

1 LB. BACON

Cut crusts from all 4 sides of bread. (Give crusts to birds!) Spread mushroom soup generously, directly from can, on each bread slice. Cut bacon strips in half. Roll bread slices diagonally, wrap bacon slice around bread roll and secure with toothpick. Bake in 350° oven 1 hour. Great for snacks, light supper with soup, or at partytime.

FAKE PATE DE FOIE GRAS

8 OZ. LIVERWURST

2 TSP. ONION, CUT FINE

1 TBSP. LEMON JUICE

1 TSP. WORCESTERSHIRE

1 TBSP. SHERRY

1 TSP. CURRY POWDER

GROUND PEPPER

2 TBSP. MAYONNAISE

Combine all ingredients thoroughly and pack into small bowl. Top with frosting and chopped pistachio nuts.

FROSTING: 3 oz. cream cheese, 2 Tbsp. milk, Pistachio nuts, chopped. Combine cream cheese and milk. Spread on above mixture and top with nuts.

REFEREE'S NOTE: *An all-star production for Mr. Tailgate.*

Q. What current quarterback was Sporting News' NFL Player of the Year in 1971? *Answer page 105.*

NATIONAL FOOD LOVERS

BRUNCH/TAILGATE

Jon Stensrud

THE KICK OFF

JOHN WAYNE'S CHEESE CASEROLE

4 - 4 OZ. CANS GREEN CHILIES, DRAINED AND DICED WITH SEEDS REMOVED

1 LB. MONTEREY JACK CHEESE, GRATED

1 LB. CHEDDAR CHEESE, GRATED

4 EGG WHITES

4 EGG YOLKS

⅔ C. CANNED EVAPORATED MILK, DILUTED

1 TBSP. FLOUR

½ TSP. SALT

⅛ TSP. PEPPER

2 MED. TOMATOES, SLICED

by JAN STENERUD
(#3, PK, Kansas City Chiefs)

In large bowl, combine the grated cheese and the chilies. Turn into a well-buttered, 2 qt. casserole. In a large bowl, beat egg whites with mixer at high speed until stiff peaks form. In small bowl, combine egg yolks, milk, flour, salt and pepper; mix until blended. Using a rubber spatula, gently fold beaten whites into yolk mixture. Pour egg mixture over cheese mixture in casserole and using a fork, ooze it through the cheese. Bake 30 mins. at 325°. Remove from oven, arrange sliced tomatoes overlapping edge. Bake 30 mins. longer, or until a silver knife inserted into center comes out clean. Serves 6-8.

REFEREE'S NOTE: This would be a terrific "kick-off" to your next tailgate party!

NOTES FROM THE BENCH: "Fantastic!"

Jan Stenerud

EARLY RISER HOT DOGS

BUTTER

HOT DOGS

WHITE WINE OR YOUR FAVORITE JUICE

by JOHN THOMPSON
(General Manager, Seattle Seahawks)

Saute hot dogs in butter, taking care to brown them without burning the butter. Add, sparingly, the wine — or if you prefer, a juice or even water. Cover and simmer for at least 10 mins. Serve immediately while hot.

REFEREE'S NOTE: You'll never be caught in a short yardage situation with this simple breakfast/brunch/tailgate recipe.

THE COACH'S SCRAMBLE

1 MED. ONION

1 LB. GROUND LAMB (OR GROUND BEEF)

DASH OF ALLSPICE

8 EGGS

SALT AND PEPPER

BUTTER

by ABE GIBRON
(Assistant Head Coach, Tampa Bay Buccaneers)

Saute onion in a little butter, add meat, dash of allspice and brown. Add well beaten eggs and cook until eggs are done. Salt and pepper to taste. Serves 6.

Abe Gibron

EMERSON BOOZER'S SAUSAGE RING

2 - 1 LB. LOAVES SAUSAGE MEAT

1½ C. SOFT BREAD CRUMBS*

¼ C. MILK

SMALL ONION, GRATED

1 APPLE, FINELY CHOPPED

*MAKE CRUMBS IN BLENDER FROM BREAD SLICES

CARRY ALONG CRUSTLESS QUICHE

8 EGGS, WELL BEATEN

1 C. LIGHT CREAM, HALF AND HALF

SALT AND PEPPER TO TASTE

10 SLICES BACON

½ LB. FRESH MUSHROOMS, THINLY SLICED, or 2 - 4 OZ. CANS MUSHROOMS

1 - 8 OZ. PKG. AMERICAN CHEESE

PARSLEY

PAPRIKA

"RAZZLE DAZZLE" CASSEROLE

4 C. COOKED RICE

¼ C. BUTTER OR MARGARINE

1 C. ONION, CHOPPED

2 C. SOUR CREAM

1 C. COTTAGE CHEESE, CREAM STYLE

1 LG. BAY LEAF

½ TSP. SALT

⅛ TSP. PEPPER

3 - 4 OZ. CANS GREEN CHILI, DRAINED

2 C. SHARP CHEDDAR CHEESE, GRATED

by EMERSON BOOZER
(Former New York Jets HB)

Mix and bake 1 hour at 350°. Use ring mold or regular baking dish and shape into form of a ring. You may scramble eggs and place in center. For added color, place fresh parsley tips on side. Serves 6.

NOTES FROM THE BENCH: *"This is basically a breakfast recipe, but could be used as main dish with other vegetables at any time. My wife likes to serve this for breakfast. Everything goes on one large platter and is placed on table. Clean up minimal."*

by PAT GRANT
(Bud Grant, Head Coach, Minnesota Vikings)

Combine beaten eggs, cream and seasonings in mixing bowl, blend well. In skillet, lightly brown bacon, remove to paper towels and drain thoroughly. Crumble bacon and add to egg mixture with sliced mushrooms. Line bottom and sides of lightly greased quiche pan or 9 x 13" baking dish with slices of American cheese. Pour egg mixture over all. Sprinkle with parsley and paprika. Bake at 350° for 30 mins. until lightly brown and puffy. Serves 4-6.

REFEREE'S NOTE: *Put this on your reserve list for a "superstar" addition to any brunch, tailgate, picnic or light supper.*

by DONNA LENKAITIS
(Bill Lenkaitis, #67, C, New England Patriots)

Pre-heat oven to 375°. Saute onion in butter until golden. Remove from heat and stir in rice, sour cream, cottage cheese, bay leaf and salt and pepper. Mix lightly. Add half the rice mixture to buttered baking dish, then add half the chili and sprinkle with 1 C. cheddar cheese. Repeat. Bake 30 mins.

REFEREE'S NOTE: *Make this "winning combination" the "center" of your next tailgating bash!*

EGGS BENEDICT A LA STEELERS

8 EGGS

8 SLICES CANADIAN BACON

WATER

1 TSP. SALT

3 TBSP. WHITE VINEGAR

4 TOASTED ENGLISH MUFFINS,
SLICED IN HALF

HOLLANDAISE SAUCE,
(RECIPE TO FOLLOW)

BLACK OLIVES, SLICED

PARSLEY

REFEREE'S NOTE: Steal the hearts of your Brunch-Bunch.

by STEVE FURNESS
(#64, DE-T, Pittsburgh Steelers)

Saute the Canadian bacon in butter. Put aside. Fill a 10"-12" frying pan one inch deep with water. Add salt and vinegar, bring to boil. Break each egg carefully into a small bowl. Slide egg slowly into boiling water and reduce heat. When eggs are firm, about 10 mins., remove from water with a slotted spoon; trim ragged whites. Put a slice of cooked Canadian bacon on each English muffin half, one of the poached eggs, cover with hollandaise sauce. Garnish with olives, parsley. Serves 8.

HOLLANDAISE SAUCE: 3 eggs yolks; 1 Tbsp. cold water; ¼ tsp. salt; ½ tsp. lemon juice; ½ C. butter, melted. Combine egg yolks, water, salt, and lemon juice in a blender. Add hot butter slowly until mixture thickens, about 20 mins.

Steve Furness

CREOLE RED BEANS AND RICE

1 THICK SLICE RAW HAM

1 SLICE PICKLED PORK

1 LB. RED KIDNEY BEANS

2 ONIONS, CHOPPED

1 BELL PEPPER, CHOPPED

3 RIBS CELERY, CHOPPED

4 GARLIC CLOVES, MINCED

1 TSP. SUGAR

2 TSP. VINEGAR

2 BAY LEAVES

½ TSP. POWDERED THYME

⅛ TSP. POWDERED ALLSPICE

⅛ TSP. POWDERED CLOVES

½ TSP. CHILI POWDER

⅛ TSP. CAYENNE PEPPER

¼ TSP. BLACK PEPPER

SALT TO TASTE

by DICK NOLAN
(Head Coach, New Orleans Saints)

In a heavy pot, put raw ham and pickled pork; cover with 2 qts. of cold water. Set the pan on low heat and while it is heating, clean the beans. Take a handful at a time and pick out the gravel, dirt, etc. Rinse the beans and add to the pot. Add onions, bell pepper, celery and garlic to the pot. Add all seasonings except salt. Add salt only after the beans have cooked for at least 3 hours. As the pot cooks, never let it boil but allow to simmer gently. As the beans begin to soften, stir the pot about 3 or 4 times an hour. Mash some of the beans against the side of the pot. The result will be a thick, creamy sauce. Serve over rice with sausages. Serves 6.

NOTES FROM THE BENCH: *"This is a traditional Monday night dinner for New Orleans' families. It sticks to your ribs!"*

Dick Nolan

BOOM-BOOM BROWN'S TAILGATE TACOS

1 C. GREEN PEPPER, SLICED

1 C. CELERY, DICED

½ C. ONION, CHOPPED

1 LB. GROUND BEEF

1 - 1⅜ OZ. PKG. CHILI SEASONING MIX

1 - 16 OZ. CAN KIDNEY BEANS

1 - 17 OZ. CAN CORN

1 - 8 OZ. CAN TOMATO SAUCE

24 TACO SHELLS

LETTUCE, SHREDDED

CHEESE, SHREDDED

by BILL BROWN
(Former Minnesota Vikings FB)

Saute celery, pepper, onion until tender. Add meat and brown. Stir in remaining ingredients and simmer uncovered for 15 mins. Spoon into shells on a bed of lettuce and top with cheese.

NOTES FROM THE BENCH; *"This recipe may be used as a "super bowl" taco dip. I put the cooked ingredients in a chafing dish and serve with corn chips."*

Bill Brown

Q. What former Viking player was involved in the "worst trade" George Halas ever made? *Answer page 105.*

WILD CARD ENCHILADAS

12 TORTILLA SHELLS

2 C. CHICKEN, COOKED

3 GREEN ONIONS, CHOPPED

LETTUCE, SHREDDED

½ LB. MONTEREY JACK CHEESE, GRATED

2 TBSP. GREEN CHILIES, CHOPPED

SAUCE:

2 C. TOMATO PUREE OR SAUCE

2 C. WATER

4 TSP. ONIONS, DICED

2 BOUILLON CUBES

1½ TSP. SALT

1 TSP. GARLIC POWDER

1 TSP. OREGANO

by MARK KONCAR
(#79, OT, Green Bay Packers)

Combine sauce ingredients and cook 5 mins. over medium heat. Fry tortilla shells in a little oil. Dip tortilla in sauce, remove and fill with all other ingredients except the cheese. Roll up tortilla and place in casserole dish. Once all tortillas are in the dish, spoon additional sauce over top. Cover with cheese. Heat at 350° for approximately 20 mins. Serves 6.

REFEREE'S NOTE: *Mark got this recipe from a fellow player, Derrel Gofourth — that's the team spirit!*

NOTES FROM THE BENCH: *"You'll like this if you are a Mexican food fan or not!"*

"BLITZ" BEAN CASSEROLE

6 SLICES BACON, COOKED

1-2 LBS. HAMBURGER, BROWNED AND DRAINED

1 ONION, BROWNED WITH HAMBURGER

AFTER HAMBURGER AND ONION ARE DONE, DRAIN EXCESS FAT.

ADD: ½ C. CATSUP

½ C. VINEGAR

1 TBSP. MUSTARD

1 CAN LIMA BEANS, DRAINED

1 LG. CAN PORK AND BEANS

BACON, BROKEN INTO BITS

by ROBBIE GROGAN
(Steve Grogan, #14, QB, New England Patriots)

Cook in oven, crock pot or electric skillet for 30 to 60 mins. to heat thoroughly, about 325°. This will freeze nicely and it's great to have on hand for emergencies.

HINT: Dribble maple syrup over bacon before broiling on rack in 250° oven for unusually delicious taste.

"NICKEL DEFENSE" CASSEROLE

2 - 7 OZ. CANS TUNA, FLAKED

2 - 16 OZ. CANS MIXED VEGETABLES, DRAINED

1 CAN CONDENSED CHICKEN SOUP

2 OZ. CHEESE, GRATED

POTATO CHIPS

by VIVIENNE SMITH
(John Smith, #1, PK, New England Patriots)

In ovenproof covered dish, layer ingredients: Tuna, 1 can; soup, ½ can; vegetables, 1 can; layer of potato chips. Repeat. Cover and cook in oven 350° for 45 mins. Uncover for last 5 mins. when grated cheese is put on to melt.

REFEREE'S NOTE: Easy on the budget.

"SUICIDE SQUAD" GARLIC PIZZA

2 LOAVES OF FROZEN BREAD

½ C. OLIVE OIL

2 CLOVES OF GARLIC, CHOPPED FINE OR PRESSED JUICE INTO OIL

½ TSP. DRIED PARSLEY

¼ TSP. OREGANO

SALT AND PEPPER

by VIVIAN NICCOLAI
(Armand Niccolai, Former Pittsburgh Pirates K)

Take 2 loaves of partly thawed frozen bread and cut into one-inch pieces on a well greased cookie sheet (one with sides). After the sheet is covered with one-inch pieces of bread, grease the dough and cover with waxed paper. Allow dough to raise overnight. Next morning, put garlic into the oil and heat to boiling point. While hot, spoon the garlic oil mixture over the bread dough. Sprinkle with oregano, parsley, salt and pepper. Bake at 350° for 45 mins. or until desired brownness. Serves 6.

REFEREE'S NOTE: No punt necessary — this pizza's a kick!

"DOUBLE COVERAGE" CHILI SAUCE

3-3½ LBS. CUBED PORK BUTT

3 TBSP. TOMATO PASTE

½ C. TOMATO SAUCE

½ C. WATER

2 CLOVES GARLIC, CHOPPED

3 - 4 TBSP. RED CHILI POWDER

1-1½ TSP. GROUND CUMIN

¼ C. SOUR CREAM

3 TBSP. BUTTER

SALT TO TASTE

¾ TSP. TARRAGON

FLOUR TORTILLAS

2 AVOCADOS

SOUR CREAM

GREEN ONIONS, CHOPPED

by RON MIX

(Hall of Fame, San Diego Chargers OT)

Saute garlic and onions over low heat until golden in color. Set aside. In same pan, saute pork until uniformly browned. Turn heat to lowest temperature and add tomato sauce, tomato paste, water, chili powder, cumin, tarragon. Let simmer 1½ to 2 hours, adding water as necessary to maintain original level of sauce. Before serving, add sour cream and salt to individual taste. Put 5-6 Tbsp. on a flour tortilla. Top with slices of avocado and chopped green onions and a dollup of sour cream. Roll up tortilla and eat it with your hands. Serves 6-8.

REFEREE'S NOTE: *Tackles any hungry appetite.*

Ron Mix

MONDAY NIGHT CHOWDER

1 - 7½ OZ. CAN KING CRAB

1 - 4½ OZ. CAN TINY SHRIMP

2 -8 OZ. CAN MINCED CLAMS

4 STRIPS BACON, DICED

1 CLOVE GARLIC, MINCED

2 C. POTATOES, DICED

1 C. DRY WHITE WINE

2 TSP. SALT

⅛ TSP. PEPPER

½ TSP. THYME

1 - 16 OZ. CAN CREAM STYLE CORN

3 C. MILK

1 C. HALF AND HALF

½ C. GREEN ONIONS, CHOPPED

2 TBSP. PARSLEY, MINCED

by RICH SAUL

(#61, C, Los Angeles Rams)

Drain crab, shrimp and clams. Reserve liquids. Slice crab with sharp knife. Cook bacon and garlic in kettle until bacon is crisp. Add potatoes, reserved seafood liquids, wine, salt, pepper and thyme. Cover and simmer 15-20 mins. or until potatoes are tender. Add crab, shrimp, clams, corn, milk, half and half, onions and parsley. Heat to simmer, do not boil. Serves 6-8.

REFEREE'S NOTE: *This would make any armchair quarterback a hero!*

Rich Saul

"SAFETY" SHRIMP AND MUSHROOMS

2 TBSP. BUTTER

2 C. CELERY, CHOPPED

1 - 16 OZ. CAN SLICED MUSHROOMS, DRAINED

1 TBSP. SOY SAUCE

1 TSP. GINGER

1 TBSP. CORNSTARCH

1 TBSP. WATER

½ C. BEEF BROTH

2 - 4½ OZ. CANS SHRIMP, DRAINED AND RINSED

2 C. HOT COOKED RICE

by SHARON CONN
(Dick Conn, #22, S, New England Patriots)

In large skillet, melt butter, cook and stir celery, mushrooms, soy sauce, ginger and pepper until celery is tender, about 5 mins. Mix cornstarch and water. Stir cornstarch mixture and broth into celery and mushrooms. Cook, stirring frequently, until mixture thickens. Stir in shrimp, heat through. Spoon each serving over ½ C. rice. Serves 4.

THE CONGRESSMAN'S FRENCH DIP

5 LBS. BOTTOM ROUND OR BEEF BRISKET

¾ LB. MONTEREY JACK CHEESE OR MUENSTER CHEESE, SLICED

EQUAL PARTS MAYONNAISE AND PICKLE RELISH

PEPPER

SALT

LAWRY'S SEASONING SALT

LONG FRENCH ROLLS
(WE LIKE SOFT STEAK ROLLS)

by JACK KEMP
(Former Buffalo Bills QB)

Brown meat in large pot. Add 4 C. water, pepper, salt and Lawry's salt. Simmer 5 or 6 hours. Remove meat and save juice. Slice meat thinly if bottom round is used. If brisket is used, pull apart with fork. Put meat back into juice and refrigerate overnight. To serve, heat in 350° oven 45 mins. or until hot. Mix mayonnaise and pickle relish and put into serving dish. Slice rolls in half and broil till lightly browned. Dip broiled side of rolls into juice briefly. Put meat on one side of roll, cheese on top and relish on other side of roll. Serves 6.

REFEREE'S NOTE: *A crowd pleaser!*

JOHNNY MASETTI CASSEROLE

1 MED. BOX NOODLES

2 LBS. GROUND PORK SAUSAGE

2 LG. ONIONS

1 CAN TOMATOES

½ LB. GRATED CHEDDAR CHEESE

2 TBSP. SUGAR

by JACK KEMP
(Former Buffalo Bills QB)

Cook noodles. Saute meat and onion. Add tomatoes, salt, pepper and sugar to meat mixture. Mix in ⅔ of cheese, then the noodles. Put into large casserole. Top with remaining cheese. Bake in 400° oven for 20 mins. or until hot.

IRISH STEW A LA GREAT GRANDMA CASSADY

6 LAMB CHOPS or 2 LBS. CUT UP LAMB

8 POTATOES, PEELED AND CUT IN HALF

2 LG. ONIONS, CUT IN ⅛'s

1 TURNIP, DICED

2 CARROTS, DICED

1 STALK CELERY, DICED

SALT, PEPPER

1 TSP. EACH: CLOVES, CINNAMON, CELERY SEED, MUSTARD

½ TEACUP CATSUP

1 TEACUP SWEET PICKLE VINEGAR

1 SLICE HAM FAT OR ¼ LB. BUTTER

1 PT. MEAT STOCK

by HOWARD CASSADY
(Former Detroit Lions, Philadelphia Eagles HB, WR)

Put in pot a layer of potatoes, 2 chops, layer onions, turnip, carrot, celery, sprinkle seasonings as you go. Add catsup, mustard, pickle vinegar to meat stock. Pour meat stock over stew. Put ham fat or butter on top of stew. Cover tightly and let simmer for 1½ hours. Watch so it does not burn. Thicken liquids with flour if needed. Serve with dumplings or hot biscuits and Guiness stout. Serves 6.

REFEREE'S NOTE. Hopalong's Great Grandma's stew is so good, it's almost unsportsmanlike!

NATIONAL FOOD LOVERS REDMOND RED CHILI

2 LBS. LEAN GROUND BEEF

1 LG. ONION, CHOPPED

1 LG. GREEN PEPPER, CHOPPED

1 LB. OR 2 - 10 OZ. CANS STEWED TOMATOES

1 LB. OR 2 - 10 OZ. CANS TOMATO SAUCE

1 SM. CAN TOMATO PASTE

1 C. WATER

1 TSP. GARLIC POWDER

4 TBSP. CUMIN

5 TBSP. CHILE POWDER

SALT AND PEPPER TO TASTE

HOT JALAPENO PEPPER, DICED (OPTIONAL)

2 - 12 OZ. CANS PINTO BEANS

1½ LBS. SMALL BUTTON MUSHROOMS

respectfully submitted by MIKE KELLER AND JOHN THOMPSON
(Assistant to the General Manager, Seattle Seahawks, and General Manager, Seattle Seahawks)

Brown meat over high heat, adding onion and green pepper. Drain off grease. Add stewed tomatoes, tomato sauce, tomato paste, water, cumin, chile powder, garlic powder, salt, pepper and if desired, jalapenos. Bring to boil, stirring occasionally. Lower heat and simmer for 15 mins. Add pinto beans and mushrooms and bring to boil again. Simmer 10 mins. and serve. Note: Those with tastes for hotter chile and with cast iron stomachs may add chile powder and jalapenos to taste. But it's best to begin mild and work up! Serves 8.

REFEREE'S NOTE: It's a "questionable call" as to the origin and originator of this delectable dish. John Thompson recalls he borrowed (stole?) this recipe from an ex-Dallas Cowboy linebacker. He comments: "I once saw Al Onofrio, the long time University of Missouri coach who is now a Seattle scout, devour six bowls of this chili — at its very hottest." Mike Keller insists his recipe was an original — modified from years of scouting through the southwest and living in Dallas.

"SQUARE OUT" TURKEY BARS

16 BREAD SLICES, OR 4 SLICES, CUT LENGTH OF LOAF

¾-1 STICK BUTTER

8 SLICES MILD CHEDDAR CHEESE

2 C. TURKEY, BITE-SIZE PIECES

¼ GREEN PEPPER

½ CAN CREAM OF MUSHROOM SOUP

½ CAN CREAM OF CHICKEN SOUP

2 TSP. ONION, MINCED

¼ TSP. SALT

¼ TSP. PAPRIKA

¼ TSP. WORCESTERSHIRE SAUCE

DASH TABASCO SAUCE

4 EGGS

1½ C. MILK

SLIVERED ALMONDS

Grease an 8x12" or 9x13" baking pan with peanut oil or Wesson oil. Remove crusts from bread slices. Butter bread on both sides and place half of the slices in baking pan. Arrange flat according to size of pan. Place cheese slices on top of bread; then spread turkey on top of cheese and place remainder of bread on top of turkey. Put green pepper, mushroom soup and chicken soup in blender and blend until smooth. Add all seasonings and mix well. Add eggs, milk; continue blending until mixed thoroughly. Pour liquid over ingredients in baking pan and sprinkle with almonds. Cover with foil and place in refrigerator overnight. Allow to come to room temperature before baking — about 1 to 1½ hours to reach room temp. Bake 1 hour at 325°, uncovered; allow to brown evenly on top. Serve hot. This may be cooled and covered with foil, placed in the freezer and used at a later date — if so, remove from freezer about 3 hours before baking and bake 1 hour at 350°, uncovered. Serves 12. Cut in bar-shaped servings, when using long bread slices. Serves 8 larger portions when using regular size bread slices cut in squares.

Q. Who was in the starting backfield for the New York Jets in the Super Bowl III? Namath, Snell, and ? *Answer page 105.*

"SAFETY BLITZ" MACARONI-CHEESE PUFF

½ C. SMALL ELBOW MACARONI

1½ C. SKIM MILK

6 OZ. SHARP AMERICAN CHEESE, SHREDDED, 1½ C.

3 BEATEN EGG YOLKS

1 C. SOFT BREAD CRUMBS, 1½ SLICES

¼ C. CHOPPED CANNED PIMENTO

2 TBSP. GREEN ONION, CHOPPED

3 EGG WHITES

¼ TSP. CREAM OF TARTAR

Cook macaroni in boiling, salted water till tender; drain. Combine milk, cheese, and ¼ tsp. salt; stir over low heat till cheese melts. Stir small amount of hot mixture into egg yolks. Return to hot mixture; blend well. Stir in macaroni, crumbs, pimento, and onion. Beat egg whites with cream of tartar till stiff. Fold into macaroni mixture. Pour into ungreased 1½ qt. souffle dish. Bake at 325° till knife inserted off-center comes out clean, about 1 hour. Serve immediately. Serves 6.

REFEREE'S NOTE: A safe, sure play at a slim 226 calories per serving.

FOR MEN ONLY — TURKEY DEVINE

1½ TSP. OLIVE OIL

4 LG. MUSHROOMS, SLICED

2 TBSP. ONION, CHOPPED

¼ C. FRESH PARSLEY

1½ C. CHICKEN BOUILLON

½ C. DRY WHITE WINE

8 OZ. PKG. MEDIUM EGG NOODLES

1 MED. SIZE CAN PIMENTO, CHOPPED

SALT AND PEPPER

8 SLICES COOKED TURKEY, 3½"
by 2½" by ¼"

Heat olive oil in a skillet and add mushrooms and chopped onion. Saute until lightly browned. Add parsley, chicken bouillon and dry white wine. Heat to boiling point, then simmer, covered for 20 mins. Meantime, cook noodles in salted boiling water until tender. Drain, then add them to the mushroom-onion mixture in skillet. Add pimento. Mix well and season with salt and pepper to taste. Arrange turkey slices over the noodle mixture. Cover and cook over low heat for 10 mins. or until turkey is thoroughly heated. Serves 4.

THE UMPIRE'S CRAB

1 - 7½ OZ. CAN CRAB MEAT, DRAINED, FLAKED AND CARTILAGE REMOVED

¼ C. LOW-CAL MAYONNAISE-TYPE DRESSING

1 OZ. AMERICAN CHEESE, SHREDDED,

¼ C. CELERY, CHOPPED FINE

1 TBSP. CHOPPED CANNED PIMENTO

2 TSP. LEMON JUICE

3 ENGLISH MUFFINS SPLIT AND TOASTED

In bowl, combine crab, dressing, cheese, celery, pimento, and lemon juice; mix well. Spread about ¼ C. of the crab mixture atop each muffin half. Broil 4 to 5 inches from heat till cheese melts, about 2-3 mins. Garnish with parsley, if desired. Serves 6.

REFEREE'S NOTE: The Ump calls this one fairly — how does 139 calories a shot sound?

JINX'S SEAFOOD CASSEROLE

1 PKG. STOUFFER'S FROZEN MACARONI AND CHEESE

1 - 10½ OZ. CAN CAMPBELL'S SHRIMP SOUP

2 - 6 OZ. PKG. FROZEN WAKEFIELD CRABMEAT AND SHRIMP

1 TBSP. DRY SHERRY

½ C. BUTTERED BREAD CRUMBS, OR MORE

CHEESE, GRATED

Thaw and break up macaroni and cheese; mix with soup in casserole. Add thawed seafood and Sherry. Mix all together very gently. Top with buttered bread crumbs and cheese. Bake at 350° for 25 mins. Serves 6 to 8.

REFEREE'S NOTE: "Blind side" your guests with this tasty casserole that any rookie could prepare — or for the serious cooks, you'll love the simple preparation and beautiful presentation this dish affords.

"A SEASONED PLAYER" SEAFOOD AND SPAGHETTI RING

8 OZ. SPAGHETTI

1 C. SWISS CHEESE, SHREDDED

1 - .6 OZ. PKG. GARLIC OR ITALIAN SALAD DRESSING MIX

¼ C. SNIPPED PARSLEY

2 TBSP. BUTTER OR MARGARINE, MELTED

½ C. ONION, FINELY CHOPPED

1 - 4 OZ. CAN SLICED MUSHROOMS, DRAINED

2 TBSP. BUTTER OR MARGARINE

1 - 15 OZ. CAN SPAGHETTI SAUCE

1 - 6½ OZ. CAN MINCED CLAMS, DRAINED

1 - 7 OZ. CAN TUNA, DRAINED AND BROKEN INTO CHUNKS

Cook spaghetti according to package directions, drain. In bowl combine spaghetti, cheese, salad dressing mix, parsley, and the melted butter or margarine; mix well. Turn mixture into a greased 4½ C. ring mold. Let stand 5 mins. Meanwhile, in saucepan cook onion and mushrooms in remaining butter about 5 mins. or until onion is tender but not brown. Add spaghetti sauce and clams, simmer 5 mins. Gently stir in tuna; heat through. Unmold spaghetti onto serving plate; serve with sauce. Serves 6.

REFEREE'S NOTE: *After a long day at the game, who needs a night over the stove?*

Q. What current professional player boxed the world heavyweight champion Muhammad Ali? *Answer page 105.*

"GOAL LINE" CHICKEN SALAD

by RON MIX
(Hall of Fame, San Diego Chargers OT)

3 LBS. CHICKEN

½ C. RAW PEANUTS OR CASHEWS

3 OZ. RICE STICKS (PY MEI FUN)

¼ C. RAW SESAME SEEDS

3 OR 4 STALKS CELERY

½ HEAD OF LETTUCE, SHREDDED

3 GREEN ONIONS, SLIVERED

1 TSP. SALT

1 TBSP. THIN SOY SAUCE

2 TSP. OYSTER SAUCE

2-3 TBSP. SESAME OIL

1 QT. OIL FOR DEEP FRYING

Boil chicken just until done, 25-30 mins. Remove from pan and let cool. Tear chicken meat into small, bite-size pieces. Heat oil to 325° and deep fry peanuts for 5 mins. Drain and chop into small pieces. Deep fry rice sticks for 2 mins. They will increase in size about 4 times. Drain and set aside. Chop celery into bite size pieces. Combine chicken, lettuce, celery and onions in a large bowl. Add salt, soy sauce, oyster sauce, and sesame oil and toss again. Just before serving, add the rice sticks, sesame seeds and peanuts. Toss again. Serves 12.

NOTES FROM THE BENCH: *"This is an ideal dinner which seems to abate hunger better than most salads, probably because of the meat content. Perfect for hot days and before or after vigorous activities."*

STAN WEST'S CHILI

2 LBS. GROUND BEEF

2 - 8 OZ. CANS TOMATO SAUCE

3 CANS WATER

1 PKG. 2-ALARM BRAND CHILI SPICES

MASA FLOUR

1 - 2 LB. PKG. KIDNEY BEANS (SOAK BEANS OVERNIGHT AND COOK SEPARATELY ACCORDING TO PACKAGE DIRECTIONS.)

by STAN WEST
(Scout, St. Louis Cardinals)

In a large skillet, brown meat and pour off excess liquid. Add tomato sauce, water and spices according to package directions. Simmer for 1½ hours. Check for consistency and add masa flour to thicken, if necessary. Allow to simmer an additional 15-20 mins. Serve alone or over beans. Serves 4 to 6.

NOTES FROM THE BENCH: *"This has been a great recipe — never a failure and that's some record."*

Stan West

"CHALK TALK" SAUSAGE AND GRITS CASSEROLE

1 LB. HOT SAUSAGE, (BULK)

1 C. HOMINY GRITS

4 C. BOILING WATER

1 TSP. SALT

½ C. MARGARINE

¼ LB. GARLIC CHEESE

½ C. MILK

3 EGGS, SLIGHTLY BEATEN

PAPRIKA

by PAT MINER
(Tom Miner, Scout, Cleveland Browns)

Fry sausage and drain well. Cook grits in boiling water 5 mins. stirring often. Add margarine and cheese, blend until melted. Remove from heat and add milk, eggs and sausage. Mix thoroughly, and pour into greased casserole, sprinkle with paprika. Bake 30-35 mins. at 350°. May be refrigerated overnight and baked next morning.

NOTES FROM THE BENCH: *"This recipe will help any Southerner survive in beautiful sunny California and even convert a few "breakfast abstainers." Delicious served with hot tortillas!"*

VICTORY CASSEROLE

9 SLICES BREAD, CAN BE A MIXTURE OF WHITE AND WHEAT

½ LB. SHREDDED CHEESE, CHEDDAR OR MIX WITH JACK CHEESE

6 EGGS

3¼ C. MILK

½ TSP. SALT

¼ TSP. PEPPER

1 TSP. DRY MUSTARD

3 STRIPS OF THICK SLICED BACON

by PAT MINER
(Tom Miner, Scout, Cleveland Browns)

Crumble bread and mix with cheese and spread in bottom of greased 7½x12" flat baking dish. Beat eggs and milk, stir in salt, pepper and mustard and pour over bread-cheese mixture. Lay strips of bacon on top. Refrigerate 4-6 hours or overnight. Bake uncovered at 350° for 55 mins. Serves 6. (Variation — ham can be chopped and included with the bread-cheese mixture.)

NOTES FROM THE BENCH: *"A perfect way to end a victory celebration, late at night, or for that really special brunch. This casserole can be prepared the day before and baked while the party is going on."*

"TRAINING TABLE" BROCCOLI OMELET

4 EGGS

½ OF 10 OZ. BOX CHOPPED FROZEN BROCCOLI

4 OZ. LONGHORN CHEESE, CUT UP

SALT AND PEPPER

2 OZ. MILK

BUTTER

by DON JOYCE

(National Scout for Blesto Scouting Combine)

Break and beat eggs in large bowl. Add thawed broccoli and rest of ingredients. Put melted butter in bottom and sides of hot omelet pan. Use half of recipe and add rest slowly. Fry until golden brown. Makes 2 omelets, serves 3-4.

NOTES FROM THE BENCH: "Serve with bacon, ham or sausage and hash browned spuds with paprika — best on Sundays!"

EDITOR'S FAMILY FAVORITE MUSHROOM STRATA

2½ C. SEASONED CROUTONS

2 C. CHEDDAR CHEESE, SHREDDED

½ LB. FRESH MUSHROOMS, SLICED

4 GREEN ONIONS, SLICED

2 TBSP. BUTTER

¾ TSP. DRY MUSTARD

2½ C. MILK

1 CAN CREAM OF MUSHROOM SOUP

½ C. MILK

4 EGGS

by CAROLYN REICHOW

Saute mushrooms and onion in butter until slightly browned. Place croutons in a greased 9x13" pan. Place cheese on top. Add mushrooms and onions, reserving ½ C. for topping. Beat egg, mustard and 2½ C. milk together. Pour over mushroom-cheese mixture. Refrigerate overnight. Next day, mix soup with remaining milk and spread over top. Sprinkle reserved mushroom mixture over casserole. Bake in a moderately slow oven, 300°, for 1½ hours. Serves 6 to 8. Note: Sausage (2 lbs.) may be added in place of mushrooms, or in addition to mushrooms.

REFEREE'S NOTE: After "serious" scouting and taste testing, the Reichow family "drafts" this mushroom strata as their first pick.

HAM AND CHEESE STRATA

12 SLICES BREAD, TRIMMED AND CUBED

1 - 10 OZ. PKG. FROZEN CHOPPED BROCCOLI, THAWED AND DRAINED

2 C. DICED HAM

2 C. CHEDDAR CHEESE, SHREDDED

6 EGGS, LIGHTLY BEATEN

3 C. MILK

2 TSP. INSTANT DRY ONIONS

½ TSP. SALT

¼ TSP. DRY MUSTARD

Cover bottom of buttered 9x13" baking pan with half the bread cubes. Layer broccoli, ham and cheese over bread; top with remaining bread cubes. Combine eggs, milk, onions, salt and mustard; pour over strata. Cover and refrigerate several hours or overnight. Bake in a 350° oven till tests done when knife inserted in center comes out clean, 55-60 mins. Let stand 10 mins. Cut into squares. Serves 8-10.

REFEREE'S NOTE: Unparalleled. Contributed by a Steelers fan who knew his strata.

OYSTER POOR BOYS

FRESH SHELLED OYSTERS
¾ C. FLOUR
¾ C. YELLOW CORN MEAL
2 TSP. SALT
2 TSP. CAYENNE PEPPER, OR TO TASTE
½ TSP. PAPRIKA
COOKING OIL
FRENCH BREAD OR ROLLS
LETTUCE
MAYONNAISE OR COCKTAIL SAUCE

by TERRY STIEVE
(#68, G, St. Louis Cardinals)

Combine flour, corn meal, salt, cayenne and paprika. Mix well. Rinse oysters, drain and pat dry. Roll oysters in batter and let absorb a few minutes. Fry oysters in hot oil until they float. Drain on paper towels. Slice French bread or rolls in half lengthwise. Make sandwiches from oysters, lettuce and mayonnaise or cocktail sauce.

REFEREE'S NOTE: Oysters — a succulent hors d'oeuvre "shows its colors" as a first round draft choice for an intriguing sandwich.

THE FIRST DOWN

ROGER STAUBACH'S SPINACH SALAD

1 BAG FRESH SPINACH, WASH, REMOVE STEMS, TEAR IN BITE-SIZE PIECES

4 OZ. BLUE CHEESE, CRUMBLED

1 CAN FRENCH FRIED ONION RINGS

DRESSING:

1 CAN TOMATO SOUP

¾ C. OIL

¾ C. VINEGAR

¾ C. SUGAR

½ TSP. SALT

1 TSP. DRY MUSTARD

¼ TSP PAPRIKA

1 ONION, GRATED

by ROGER STAUBACH

(#12, QB, Dallas Cowboys)

In a tall bottle, mix dry ingredients. Then all liquid ingredients, mixing well. Put onion in for flavor, but remove before serving. Makes enough for 2 bags of spinach.

REFEREE'S NOTE: *Fabulous fare for the first down.*

"PILING ON"

½ BUNCH SPINACH, TORN IN PIECES

SALT AND PEPPER TO TASTE

½ TSP. SUGAR

6 HARD BOILED EGGS, FINELY CHOPPED

½ LB. HAM, JULIENNE STRIPS

1 SM. HEAD ICEBERG LETTUCE, TORN OR SHREDDED

SALT AND PEPPER TO TASTE

½ TSP. SUGAR

1 PKG. FROZEN PEAS, THAWED NOT COOKED

1 MED. BERMUDA ONION, THINLY SLICED

1 C. SOUR CREAM

1 PT. MAYONNAISE

½ LB. SWISS CHEESE, JULIENNE STRIPS

½ LB. BACON , CRISPLY COOKED AND CRUMBLED

by JACK CHRISTIANSEN

(Hall of Fame, Detroit Lions DB)

Drain everything well. In bottom of large glass or wooden bowl, spread spinach. Sprinkle with salt and pepper and sugar. Add layer of eggs. Add layer of ham. Add layer of lettuce. Sprinkle with salt, pepper and sugar. Scatter peas all over. Pull onion slices into rings and spread into salad. Mix sour cream and mayonnaise and spread evenly over top. Arrange cheese over all. Cover bowl with plastic and refrigerate overnight. Just before serving, add bacon. Do not toss. Cut portion all way to bottom of bowl. For main course, use tuna, crab, shrimp, chicken or lobster for bacon. Serves 6-8.

REFEREE'S NOTE: *This substantial salad is just right for a marathon picnic or post-tailgating party.*

"THE SNAP" POTATO SALAD

AMOUNT OF POTATOES DESIRED
SPANISH ONIONS, SLICED THIN
PEPPER
M.S.G.
SMALL CURD COTTAGE CHEESE
HELLMAN'S MAYONNAISE

by RON ERHARDT
(Head Coach, New England Patriots)

Cook, peel and slice potatoes, alternate in layers potatoes, onion, salt, pepper, M.S.G., small curd cottage cheese, Hellman's mayonnaise until serving bowl is filled, ending with the mayonnaise spread to edges to seal flavor in. Cover with Saran Wrap. Refrigerate for 3 days — untouched. Ready for use.

REFEREE'S NOTE: A great make-ahead to impress your Gourmet Group at a tailgate or picnic.

Ronald Erhardt

"GAME BALL" POTATO SALAD

6 MED. POTATOES
1 C. SOUR CREAM
1 C. MAYONNAISE
2 TBSP. FLOUR
2 TBSP. GREEN ONION, MINCED
SALT TO TASTE
4-6 HARD BOILED EGGS, SLICED
¼ C. MELTED MARGARINE
BREAD CRUMBS

by DONNA MC KAY
(Bob McKay, # 66, T, New England Patriots)

Peel and slice potatoes. Cook in small amount of water until tender. Drain. Sprinkle 1 Tbsp. bread crumbs into greased 2 qt. casserole. Combine sour cream, mayonnaise, flour, onions, and blend thoroughly. Place layer of potatoes in casserole, salt, and add layer of egg slices. Spread with layer of sour cream mixture. Repeat layers. Sprinkle remaining crumbs on top and pour margarine on top. Bake at 350° for 25-45 mins. Sprinkle with crumbled bacon, if desired. This can be made ahead of time.

REFEREE'S NOTE: A special non-traditional addition to backyard cuisine.

"ONE HANDER" SNOWBALL SALAD

1 C. BOILING WATER
1 - 3 OZ. PKG. STRAWBERRY GELATIN
½ C. PORT, OR OTHER SWEET RED WINE OR CRANBERRY COCKTAIL
¼ C. COLD WATER
1 - 3 OZ. PKG. CREAM CHEESE, SOFTENED
⅓ C. NUTS, FINELY CHOPPED
1 TBSP. SUGAR
2 C. STRAWBERRIES

by BETTY HASSELBECK
(Don Hasselbeck, #80, TE, New England Patriots)

Pour boiling water over gelatin in bowl, stirring until gelatin is dissolved. Stir in wine and cold water. Chill until slightly thickened, but not set. Shape cream cheese into 18 balls, roll each in nuts. Sprinkle sugar over strawberries; mix gently. Pour ⅓ C. thickened gelatin into 6 cup ring mold. Arrange cheese balls evenly in gelatin. Spoon in sweetened strawberries over the cheese balls and gelatin. Pour remaining thickened gelatin carefully over berries. Chill until firm. Garnish with strawberries.

REFEREE'S NOTE: This is a sweet catch. Could be used as a sumptuous strawberry dessert.

RON KRAMER'S CAESAR SALAD

2 HEADS OF ROMAINE LETTUCE
¼ C. WINE VINEGAR
¼ C. ITALIAN OLIVE OIL
½ TSP. DRY MUSTARD
1 TSP. WORCESTERSHIRE SAUCE
2 EGGS
½ TSP. GARLIC
1 CAN ANCHOVY
½ LEMON, SQUEEZED
¼ TSP. GROUND PEPPER
3 TBSP. PARMESAN CHEESE
CROUTONS

by RON KRAMER
(Former TE, Green Bay Packers and Detroit Lions)

Clean 2 heads of romaine lettuce, wrap in towel for 2 hours. Put all other ingredients except eggs and croutons in blender and mix. When ingredients are blended sufficiently, pour into a very large bowl. Coddle 2 eggs and then add to ingredients and mix. Break lettuce with hands, do not cut!, and mix with the ingredients. Add croutons, cracked pepper and Parmesan cheese to your liking. Serves 6-8.

NOTES FROM THE BENCH: *"I use this recipe to impress guests who still think we are dumb, uncouth jocks."*

Ron Kramer

"STRONGSIDE" SICILIAN SALAD

RIPE TOMATOES, SLICED
RED ONION, SLICED THINLY
CUCUMBER, PEELED AND SLICED
WINE VINEGAR
OLIVE OIL
SALT
BLACK PEPPER, FRESH GROUND
OREGANO

by GEORGE PERNICANO
(Part-owner, San Diego Chargers)

Arrange tomato, onion and cucumber slices on a plate or in individual salad bowls. Combine vinegar, olive oil (proportion ¾ vinegar to ¼ oil). Add salt and pepper taste. Pour dressing over salad, then sprinkle with oregano to taste.

REFEREE'S NOTE: *"Strongside" temptation with this splendid low calorie dish.*

BENGAL'S BEAN SOUP

2 LBS. GREAT NORTHERN WHITE BEANS
2 HAM HOCKS, MEATY
2 CARROTS, GRATED
2 ONIONS, CHOPPED
1 C. CATSUP
1 TSP. THYME
SALT, PEPPER TO TASTE

by BOB JOHNSON
(Former Cincinnati Bengals OC)

Soak beans overnight. Cook slowly with ham hocks for several hours, adding ingredients in order given. Always have beans covered with water. Cook until done, beans are soft. Serves 15.

REFEREE'S NOTE: No "outside threat" with this soup — it's homemade.

SENIOR BOWL GUMBO

1 LG. ONION, CHOPPED

1 LG. BELL PEPPER, CHOPPED

1 C. CELERY, DICED

4 TBSP. LARD

4 TBSP. FLOUR, PLAIN AND UNSIFTED

2 CLOVES GARLIC, MINCED

4 BOUILLON CUBES, BEEF OR CHICKEN

3 QTS. WATER, BOILING

1 QT. OYSTERS

1 TBSP. "FILE" POWDER

SALT AND PEPPER TO TASTE, RED
PEPPER IF SO DESIRED

as served by WINTZELL'S OYSTER HOUSE

Brown sifted flour in lard, to a golden brown, stirring constantly to prevent burning or lumping. Add ½ chopped vegetables and garlic to brown flour and saute for about 1 min. Add this mixture to the 3 qts. of boiling water and mix thoroughly, add remaining vegetables, garlic and bouillon cubes, boil for about 10 mins. Put in oysters and simmer for at least 30 mins. Salt and pepper to taste. Then bring to rapid boil, add "file". Mix well, take off heat. Let set for at least 15 mins. Serve over boiled rice. This can be used for the basis of any seafood gumbo.

REFEREE'S NOTE: This gastronomic gumbo is a favorite of scouts and other football personalities when down in Mobile, Alabama, for the Senior Bowl.

"OFF SIDES" WINE SALAD

2½ C. BOILING WATER

1 PKG. CHERRY JELLO

1 PKG. LEMON JELLO

1 - 16 OZ. CAN DARK SWEET CHERRIES, PITTED

½ C. RED WINE

½ C. SWEET RED WINE

Dissolve jello in boiling water. Add cherries, juice and wine. Pour in ring mold. Chill. Serve with dressing in center:
½ pt. whipping cream
1 - 3 oz. pkg. cream cheese
8 lg. marshmallows, cut up
Whip cream and cheese together. Fold in marshmallows. Chill.

REFEREE'S NOTE: "Off sides" call? The ref is sure to change his mind!

GREEN GODDESS DRESSING

½ PT. CULTURED SOUR CREAM

JUICE OF 1 LEMON

2 CAN ANCHOVIES, (OIL AND ALL)

1 MED. ONION

2 SMALL BUNCHES PARSLEY

½ TSP. SALT

FRESH GROUND PEPPER TO TASTE

1 QT. HELLMAN'S MAYONNAISE

In a blender, blend well and fold into a bowl containing 1 qt. Hellman's mayonnaise. This makes 1½ qts. of dressing.

GOLDEN CHEESE SOUP

¼ C. WATER

2 TBSP. BUTTER

1 - 10 OZ. PKG. FROZEN WHOLE KERNEL CORN

½ C. SHREDDED CARROT OR PARSNIP

¼ C. ONION, CHOPPED

⅛ TSP. PEPPER

2 - 10½ OZ. CANS CONDENSED CREAM OF POTATO SOUP

2 C. MILK

1 C. CHEDDAR CHEESE, SHREDDED, 4 OZ.

½ C. PROVOLONE CHEESE, SHREDDED, 2 OZ.

1 C. BROCCOLI FLOWERETS, TINY, RAW (OPTIONAL)

Bring water, butter, corn, carrot, onion and pepper to boil in 3 qt. saucepan; cover and simmer 10 mins. Stir in soup, then milk, cheddar cheese and Provolone cheese. Heat, stirring occasionally, until cheese melts and serving temperature is reached. Do not boil. Garnish with broccoli flowerets, if desired. Yields 7-8 cups.

REFEREE'S NOTE: Ladle up a cup or two of this inviting soup at a convivial feast. A cheesy contender for the "Super" bowl.

"ORANGE CRUSH" MANDARIN MOLD

2 C. HOT WATER

1 PKG. LEMON GELATIN

1 PKG. ORANGE GELATIN

1½ C. COLD WATER

JUICE OF 1 LEMON

1 C. CRUSHED PINEAPPLE, DRAINED

1 LG. CAN MANDARIN ORANGES

30 SMALL MARSHMALLOWS

TOPPING:

2 TBSP. FLOUR

½ C. SUGAR

1 EGG, BEATEN

1 C. ORANGE JUICE

2 TBSP. BUTTER

1 C. WHIPPED CREAM

1 C. CHEDDAR CHEESE, GRATED

Pour boiling water over gelatin; stir to dissolve and add cold water and lemon juice. Let cool until it starts to congeal. Add fruit and marshmallows. Pour into 9x13" pan. Chill until firm. Topping: Mix in heavy saucepan the flour and sugar. Add egg and juice. Cook, stirring constantly, over medium heat until thick. Add butter and cool. Fold in whipped cream. Spread topping on gelatin and sprinkle with cheddar cheese. Serves 10-12.

REFEREE'S NOTE: Contributed by a wild Bronco fan who knew what Orange Crush is all about.

CHICKEN-ARTICHOKE BOWL

¾ C. LOW-CAL RUSSIAN SALAD DRESSING

2 TBSP. WATER

4 THIN SLICES ONION, SEPARATED INTO RINGS

1 CLOVE GARLIC, CRUSHED

¼ TSP. CELERY SEED

½ TSP. SALT

DASH PEPPER

1 - 9 OZ. PKG. FROZEN ARTICHOKE HEARTS

1 - 2 OZ. JAR PIMENTOS, DRAINED AND CHOPPED (¼ C.)

3 LG. CHICKEN BREASTS, SKINNED, BONED, COOKED AND CHILLED (ABOUT 2 LBS.)

2 C. EACH TORN LETTUCE, TORN ROMAINE, AND TORN FRESH SPINACH.

In medium saucepan combine salad dressing, water, onion, garlic, celery seed, salt and pepper. Bring to boiling; add frozen artichoke hearts. Cook hearts till tender, about 3 to 5 mins. Stir in chopped pimento; chill. Cut chilled chicken into cubes. At serving time drain chilled artichoke mixture, reserving marinade. Mix artichoke mixture with chicken cubes, torn greens, and enough of the reserved marinade to coat greens. Toss lightly. Serves 6.

REFEREE'S NOTE: *The odds will be with you with this delightful salad — a slight 245 calories per serving!*

Q. Who was the famous "Alley Oop" pass named after and with which team did he play? *Answer page 105.*

CREAM SOUP FROM THE BLENDER

1 C. MILK

½ C. LIGHT CREAM

1 C. CHICKEN BROTH

3 TBSP. MARGARINE

2 TBSP. FLOUR

1 TSP. SALT

¼ TSP. WHITE PEPPER

1 TSP. WORCESTERSHIRE SAUCE

1 TBSP. SHERRY

1 C. COOKED BROCCOLI, ASPARAGUS, CARROTS, CAULIFLOWER, CORN, GREEN BEANS, OR MIXED VEGETABLES

Put ingredients in blender for 30 seconds. Heat and serve.

REFEREE'S NOTE: *A tribute to the blender.*

TAILGATE COLE SLAW SALAD

1 SMALL PKG. LEMON FLAVORED GELATIN

1 C. HOT WATER

½ C. MAYONNAISE

½ C. WATER

2 TBSP. VINEGAR

¼ TSP. SALT

1½ C. CABBAGE, FINELY SHREDDED

½ C. RADISH, SLICED

½ C. CELERY, DICED

2 TBSP. GREEN PEPPER, DICED

1 TBSP. ONION, DICED

Dissolve gelatin in hot water. Blend in mayonnaise, vinegar and salt. Chill until partially set. Beat until fluffy. Add remaining ingredients. Pour into 1 qt. mold. Chill until set. Unmold on lettuce and garnish with radish slices.

REFEREE'S NOTE: *With an agile wrist and split-second timing on your slicing, dicing and shredding, you'll master a great dish for the tailgate.*

CRAB SOUP

1 CAN TOMATO SOUP

1 CAN GREEN PEA SOUP

2 CANS WATER

1 CAN CRAB MEAT

½ C. SHERRY

DASH WORCESTERSHIRE SAUCE

Combine soups and water. Add crab, Sherry and Worcestershire sauce. Heat and serve.

REFEREE'S NOTE: *Do wonderful things to your tastebuds.*

BUSY DAY VEGETABLE SOUP

½ LB. GROUND BEEF

½ BAY LEAF

1 C. TOMATO JUICE

1 LARGE CARROT, SLICED

2 RIBS CELERY, SLICED

1 ONION, CHOPPED

¼ C. RICE

1½ TSP. SALT

⅛ TSP. PEPPER

2 BOUILLON CUBES

Brown meat and drain off fat. Add bay leaf and tomato juice. Bring to a boil, and simmer for 20 mins. Add rest of ingredients and simmer 20 more mins. until vegetables are tender. Makes 4 cups.

REFEREE'S NOTE: *A welcomed oasis at the end of a trying game or day.*

HINT: To de-salt oversalted soup, slice raw potato into it and allow to boil for a few minutes; remove potato.

CRUNCHY CHINESE CABBAGE SALAD

4 C. CHINESE CABBAGE, SHREDDED

1 - 5 OZ. CAN WATER CHESTNUTS, SLICED

1 - 4 OZ. CAN MUSHROOMS, SLICED

1 TBSP. ONION, CHOPPED

½ C. MAYONNAISE

1-2 TBSP. SOY SAUCE

¾ C. CHOW MEIN NOODLES

TOASTED ALMONDS, IF DESIRED

In a large bowl, combine first 4 ingredients. Combine mayonnaise and soy sauce; pour over cabbage mixture. Toss lightly. Just before serving, add Chow Mein noodles and toss lightly. Serve immediately. If desired, garnish with toasted almonds. Serves 8-10.

REFEREE'S NOTE: A crunchy combination and an intriguing mix of textures — crunch it, you'll like it.

"EXTRA EFFORT" CREAM OF MUSHROOM SOUP

3 TBSP. BUTTER

1 SM. SLICE ONION, FINELY CHOPPED

¼ LB. FRESH MUSHROOM CAPS OR STEMS FROM ½ LB., FINELY CHOPPED

2 TBSP. FLOUR

2 CHICKEN BOUILLON CUBES, DISSOLVED IN ½ C. BOILING WATER

2 C. MILK

SALT AND PEPPER TO TASTE

½ C. CREAM OR HALF AND HALF

WHIPPED CREAM AND PARSLEY FOR GARNISH

Melt butter in top of double boiler. Add onion and mushrooms. Cook slowly for 15 mins., stirring as needed. Add flour and stir well until blended. Dissolve bouillon cubes in water and add to milk, then add slowly to mushroom mixture. Bring to boiling point and cook in double boiler for 20 mins. Season to taste. Just before serving, add cream and reheat. Garnish with whipped cream and parsley. Serves 6 small servings. Note: Dry Sherry and a sprinkling of nutmeg may be added.

REFEREE'S NOTE: With a little extra effort, you'll be a winner serving homemade, delicious mushroom soup.

AVOCADO SOUP

1 RIPE AVOCADO, PEELED

2 C. CHICKEN BROTH

1 C. LIGHT CREAM

2 TBSP. WHITE RUM

½ TSP. CURRY POWDER

½ TSP. SALT

JUICE OF 1 LIME

FRESHLY GROUND PEPPER TO TASTE

CHOPPED CHIVES

Put all ingredients in blender except chives. Blend until creamy; chill. Serve with a sprinkling of finely chopped chives on top. Yields 3 C. Serve cold.

REFEREE'S NOTE: Sipped at a "souper" tailgate in sunny San Diego.

DON JOYCE'S CREOLE GUMBO

1 FRYER

3 ONIONS, CHOPPED

2 BELL PEPPERS, CHOPPED

1 LG. CAN TOMATOES

3 PODS GARLIC, CHOPPED

4 QTS. WATER

1 LB. SLICED ANDOUILLE (CREOLE SMOKED SAUSAGE) OR HAM HOCKS OR BACON

SALT AND PEPPER

¼ LB. BUTTER OR MARGARINE

1 CAN OKRA

4 TBSP. FLOUR

4 BAY LEAVES

by DON JOYCE
(National Scout for Blesto Scouting Combine)

Make Roux (dark), in heavy Dutch oven by browning flour in butter. Keep stirring. Add water to dark brown roux. Add everything but can of okra. Cook until chicken is done. Add okra and cook 5 more mins. Serve over cooked rice in soup bowl. Note: You can add any of following or all! Shrimp - Oysters - Crabs (add last 10 mins.) Serves 4-6.

REFEREE'S NOTE: *This hearty gumbo will send your tastebuds on a trip to the Louisiana Bayou.*

"RED'S" CRANBERRY-RASPBERRY SALAD

1 - 6 OZ. PKG. RASPBERRY JELLO

1 - 3 OZ. PKG. LEMON JELLO

3 C. BOILING WATER

2 C. COLD WATER

⅓ C. PINEAPPLE JUICE

⅓ C. RASPBERRY JUICE (RESERVED FROM DRAINED JUICES)

1 - 10 OZ. PKG. FROZEN RASPBERRIES, THAWED AND DRAINED

1 - 11 OZ. CAN MANDARIN ORANGES, DRAINED

1 - 20 OZ. CAN PINEAPPLE CHUNKS, DRAINED

½ C. CELERY, FINELY CHOPPED

½ C. PECAN HALVES

1 - 14 OZ. JAR CRANBERRY ORANGE RELISH

MAYONNAISE

by NANCY MILLER
(Red Miller, Head Coach, Denver Bronco)

Combine raspberry and lemon flavored gelatins, add boiled water and stir until dissolved. Add cold water and juices and stir. Chill until partially set. Add remaining ingredients except mayonnaise, and gently stir. Pour into mold that has been lightly greased with salad oil. Chill until firm. Unmold and serve with mayonnaise.

THE BIG PLAY

Fran Tarkenton

TARKENTON'S BONED
LEG OF LAMB

BONED BUTTERFLIED LEG OF LAMB,
ALL FAT OFF

MARINADE:

½ BOTTLE BBQ SAUCE

½ BOTTLE ITALIAN DRESSING

by FRAN TARKENTON
(Sportscaster for ABC, Former Minnesota Vikings QB)

Marinate overnight. Cook on charcoal grill in basket, as for fish.

NOTES FROM THE BENCH: *"I enjoy using the charcoal grill. This is something a little out of the ordinary hamburger and steak routine."*

Fran Tarkenton

LES RICHTER'S VEAL
PARMIGIANA RAMS STYLE

6 - 6 OZ. SLICES VEAL, CUT ½" THICK

2 EGGS

SALT, PEPPER

¼ C. SAUTERNE

1 C. DRY GRATED PARMESAN CHEESE

ABOUT 1 C. FLOUR

2 TBSP. OIL

2 TBSP. BUTTER OR MARGARINE

1 C. MOZZARELLA CHEESE, GRATED

BREAD CRUMBS

TOMATO SAUCE

BELOW LINE INGREDIENTS:

GARLIC

PARSLEY

WHOLE TOMATOES

MUSHROOMS

by LES RICHTER
(Former All-Pro Los Angeles Rams MLB)

Pound veal slices thin, then beat eggs with ½ tsp. salt, a dash of pepper and the wine until mixed. Combine the bread crumbs, Parmesan cheese and season again with salt and pepper. Flour the veal by dipping in egg mixture, then in seasoned bread crumbs. Put it in freezer to chill for 30 mins. Heat oil in bottom of large skillet until it melts. Add veal and cook until golden brown on both sides. Place veal in well greased baking dish. Sprinkle mozzarella cheese over meat. For extra pleasure or taste wishes, add tomato sauce or all of the bottom line ingredients (amounts to individual liking). Bake at 350° for 15 to 20 mins. till it browns a bit.

NOTES FROM THE BENCH: *"I love veal and this basic dish allows one to have a delicious start to a good veal parmigiana with one's bottom line selections. Especially good with a California red wine."*

TERRY BARR'S HAM LOAF

1 LB. SMOKED HAM

1 LB. PORK

14 SODA CRACKER SQUARES

1 EGG

1½ C. MILK

¼ TSP. PEPPER

FETTUCINE DI BAFFI

1 LB. FETTUCINE

½ C. CREAM

¼ C. MELTED BUTTER

2-4 TBSP. GRATED ROMANO OR PARMESAN CHEESE

4-5 TBSP. RICOTTA CHEESE

1 EGG, BEATEN

PRESS BOX CHICKEN

1 - 3 LB. CUT-UP BROILER/FRYER CHICKEN

3 C. SOY SAUCE

2 TBSP. LEMON JUICE

¼ TSP. ONION POWDER

¼ TSP. GARLIC POWDER

¼ TSP. POULTRY SEASONING

¼ TSP. POWDERED GINGER

1 - 8 OZ. PKG. NOODLES

NOTES FROM THE BENCH: "Since the Intermediate Eater column began appearing in The Post-Intelligencer, I have received awards of merit from the Garlic Growers of America, The Numb Tongue Society of Chili Pepper Lovers, and from the Amalgamated Sen-Sen Corporation. It has not turned my head, only my stomach."

by TERRY BARR
(Former Detroit Lions WR-DB)

Buy ham and pork ground together from your best meat market. Mix ground meat with rolled cracker crumbs, add beaten egg, milk and pepper. Bake in meatloaf pan for 1 hour, 15 mins. at 325°.

NOTES FROM THE BENCH: *"Nothing fancy, just good food. Business takes me out so much that I prefer this type of meal at home."*

by GEORGE PERNICANO
(Part-owner, San Diego Chargers)

Cook fettucine in boiling salted water to which a dash of oil has been added. When fettucine has been cooked "al dente" (firm and a bit sticky on the teeth), drain it quickly and place in a large serving bowl. Add all the remaining ingredients. The heat of the fettucine will cook the egg and cheese into a delicious sauce.

REFEREE'S NOTE: *Redefining the spread formation!*

by JOHN OWEN
(Sports Editor, Seattle Post-Intelligencer)

Place chicken pieces skin side down in baking pan. In small mixing bowl, combine next 6 ingredients, mix well, and pour contents over chicken pieces. Flip chicken, skin side up, and bake at 375° for about 75 mins., basting twice with pan juice. When chicken is almost done, cook enough noodles to serve four in boiling water; drain well. Remove chicken to warm serving platter. Dump noodles into pan juice and "moosh" around in soy mixture. "Gloop" the noodles with sauce into serving dish. Top with chicken pieces and garnish with parsley sprigs. Serves 4.

"THE MAD SCRAMBLE" CHICKEN ORIENTAL

1 LB. BONELESS CHICKEN BREASTS, CUT IN 2" STRIPS

2 TBSP. OIL

2 CANS CAMPBELL'S CHICKEN BROTH

½ C. REGULAR RICE, UNCOOKED

¼ C. SHERRY

2 TBSP. SOY SAUCE

1 CLOVE GARLIC, MINCED

¼ TSP. GROUND GINGER

1 - 10 OZ. FROZEN BROCCOLI CUTS, PARTIALLY THAWED

1 SM. ONION, CHOPPED

1 - 8 OZ. CAN BAMBOO SHOOTS, DRAINED

¼ C. CORNSTARCH

½ C. WATER

by HAROLD CARMICHAEL
(#17, WR, Philadelphia Eagles)

In large pan, lightly brown chicken in oil. Add broth, rice, Sherry, soy sauce, onion, garlic and ginger. Bring to boil, reduce heat. Cover, simmer 15 mins. Add remaining ingredients and simmer 8 mins. Stir occasionally. Combine water and cornstarch until smooth. Stir into chicken. Cook, stirring until thickened. Serves 3-4.

REFEREE'S NOTE: This one dish meal will keep you "in motion," but you'll gain plenty of yardage with it.

Harold Carmichael

HINT: Turn a colander upside down over a frying pan when frying chicken, fish or meat. Steam can escape, but fat won't spatter.

"MY WIFE'S FRIED CHICKEN"

1 - 3 LB. FRYER, CUT UP

SALT, PEPPER, RED PEPPER, GARLIC POWDER

1 C. ALL-PURPOSE FLOUR

OIL FOR FRYING, CRISCO

NOTES FROM THE BENCH: "Eat until full — then stop (smile)."

by KEN HOUSTON
(#27, DB, Washington Redskins)

Sprinkle both sides of chicken generously with salt, black and red pepper (sparingly), and garlic powder. Place flour in a plastic bag. Add chicken, a few pieces at a time, and shake to coat well. Pour enough oil in black cast iron skillet to fill half full. Heat until waves appear in the oil, 370° in a deep fat fryer or using a frying thermometer. Place chicken in hot oil, skin side down. When underside of chicken begins to brown, turn heat down and partially cover with a lid. Turn chicken after 15 mins. or after completely browned on underside. Continue cooking, uncovered, until second side is browned. Drain thoroughly on paper towel before serving.

Kenneth D. Houston

"TITLE CLINCHING" COMPANY LAMB CHOPS

4 LOIN OR RIB LAMB CHOPS, 1" THICK

4 THIN ONION SLICES

4 SLICES SWISS CHEESE

Turn on broiler to 550°. Broil lamb chops 4 to 5 inches from heat, 7 to 8 mins. Turn. Place onion and cheese slice on each chop. Broil 7 to 8 mins. longer. Serves 4.

GAME PLAN: ROCK CORNISH HEN

ROCK CORNISH HEN

WILD RICE

CELERY

GREEN PEPPERS

ONIONS

MUSHROOMS

ALMONDS

HONEY MUSTARD

BUTTER OR MARGARINE

"DOUBLE TEAMING" CHICKEN AND RICE SUPREME

4 CHICKEN BREASTS, DEBONED AND CUT UP

½ TSP. GINGER

2 TBSP. SHERRY

1½ TBSP. CORNSTARCH

MIX ABOVE 3 INGREDIENTS AND MARINATE 7 MINS.

1 CARROT, THINLY SLICED

1 GREEN PEPPER, THINLY SLICED

1 GREEN ONION, CHOPPED

1 - 4 OZ. CAN MUSHROOMS

½ C. CASHEWS

SAUCE: ¼ TSP. GINGER

¼ TSP. GARLIC POWDER

½ TSP. SALT

¼ TSP. PAPRIKA

1 TBSP. SOY SAUCE

3 TBSP. WATER

1½ TBSP. SHERRY

¼ TSP. ACCENT

1½ TBSP. CORNSTARCH, ENOUGH TO THICKEN

by RON KRAMER
(Former Green Bay Packer TE)

Select Rock Cornish Hen from any frozen food department. Wild rice is sometimes difficult to purchase; you might have to go to the gourmet department. To make wild rice stuffing, boil rice as directed on package, simmer vegetables to your liking. I particularly like celery, green onions, mushrooms and almonds. When wild rice and vegetables are simmered, mix and stuff the Rock Cornish Hen and bake in oven at 400° for 1 to 1½ hours, basting your bird every 20 mins. with honey, mustard and butter or margarine mixed together. Serves 1.

NOTES FROM THE BENCH: *"Candlelight will make for a romantic evening."*

Ron Kramer

by LYLE ALZADO
(#77, DE, Cleveland Browns)

Cook chicken in oil until all redness is gone. Add vegetables and heat through — should remain crisp. Add sauce and stir till thick. Add cashews. Serve over long cooking rice, 1 cup. Serves 4-6.

REFEREE'S NOTE: *What a little team work will produce!*

SHRIMP CREOLE A LA KELLER

1½ LB. COOKED SHRIMP

⅓ C. BUTTER OR MARGARINE

1 MED. ONION, FINELY CHOPPED

1 C. CELERY, FINELY CHOPPED

1 SM. CAN TOMATO PASTE

2 C. TOMATO JUICE

2 TSP. SALT

½ C. TOMATO JUICE

½ TSP. CELERY SALT

½ TSP. GARLIC POWDER

½ LB. FRESH MUSHROOMS, SLICED AND SAUTEED IN 1 TBSP. BUTTER

1 GREEN PEPPER, SAUTEED IN 1 TBSP. BUTTER

¼ TSP. BAKING SODA

by MIKE KELLER
(Assistant to General Manager, Seattle Seahawks)

Melt butter or margarine, add onion and celery and cook 5 mins. Add tomato paste combined with 2 C. tomato juice and salt. Add 3 Tbsp. cornstarch dissolved in ½ C. of tomato juice. Add celery salt and garlic powder. Cook 15 mins. in covered sauce pan and add sauteed mushrooms, green pepper and cooked shrimp. Add baking soda and simmer several mins. Serve on rice. Serves 4-6.

REFEREE'S NOTE: With a flavorful recipe for shrimp like this, who wouldn't want to be a seahawk?

"DECLINE OF PENALTY" SOLE AND MUSHROOMS

¼ LB. MUSHROOMS, CLEANED AND SLICED

2 TBSP. BUTTER

1 LB. FILLET OF SOLE, THAWED OR FRESH

¼ C. DRY WHITE WINE

2 TBSP. WATER

2 TBSP. LEMON JUICE

1 TBSP. CHOPPED PARSLEY

½ TSP. DRY MUSTARD

½ TSP. SALT

¼ TSP. PEPPER

REFEREE'S NOTE: No penalty with this — it's only 192 calories per serving!

by DENNIS LICK
(#70, OT, Chicago Bears)

Lightly brown mushrooms in skillet in butter. Set aside. Wipe fillet of sole with clean damp cloth. Place in 2 qt. greased casserole. Spoon mushrooms over fillets. Blend last 7 ingredients and pour over mushrooms. Cover casserole. Bake at 375° for 25-30 mins. or until fish flakes. Serves 4. Note: Cod, flounder, perch, pike or haddock may be used instead of sole.

NOTES FROM THE BENCH: "I enjoy cooking and we like fish. This is an easy dish for any occasion."

A CORNERBACK'S CHINESE CHICKEN

4 BONELESS CHICKEN BREASTS

1 CAN PEA PODS OR FRESH

1 MED. ONION, CHOPPED

1 - 4 OZ. PKG. CASHEWS, CHOPPED

1 CAN WATER CHESTNUTS

COOKING OIL

MARINADE: 1 TSP. SALT

1 TBSP. CORNSTARCH

2 TBSP. SOY SAUCE

¼ C. CHICKEN BROTH

WHITE PEPPER

by BOBBY BRYANT
(#20, CB, Minnesota Vikings)

Marinate chicken pieces in soy marinade in refrigerator for 1 hour. Saute chicken pieces in oil in wok. Remove when done, saute onions, pea pods and water chestnuts in remaining oil. Add chicken to vegetables, add cashews and pour over sauce. Delicious served over rice or chow mein noodles.

"FLANKER" STEAK

¼ BOTTLE SOY SAUCE

1 TBSP. WORCESTERSHIRE SAUCE

½ LEMON, SQUEEZED OVER STEAK

¾ TSP. DRY MUSTARD

by BETSY HASSELBECK
(Don Hasselbeck, #80, TE, New England Patriots)

Score steak on both sides. Marinate 6-8 hours, turning frequently. Broil 8 mins. on each side. Slice paper thin.

FOWL PLAY

5 CHICKEN BREASTS

1 MED. ONION, CHOPPED

1 STALK CELERY, CHOPPED

2 - 10 OZ. PKGS. FROZEN BROCCOLI

1 C. MAYONNAISE

2 CANS OF CREAM OF CHICKEN SOUP, UNDILUTED

1 TSP. LEMON JUICE

½ C. CHEDDAR CHEESE, GRATED

½ C. BREAD CRUMBS

1 TSP. MELTED BUTTER

by PETER CRONAN
(#57, LB, Seattle Seahawks)

Simmer chicken in water until tender. Remove meat from bones and tear into narrow pieces. Cook, drain, arrange broccoli in 9x12" baking dish. Place chicken over broccoli. Combine celery, onion, mayonnaise, soup and lemon juice. Pour over chicken, sprinkle grated cheese over top, then buttered bread crumbs. Bake at 350° for 25-30 mins., until golden brown. Serves 6.

REFEREE'S NOTE: *This bill of fare won't "foul" up your budget.*

"OPTION PLAY" BAKED PHEASANT

4 HALVED PHEASANT BREASTS, BONED IF PREFERRED

SALT AND PEPPER

½ C. BUTTER

1 SM. ONION, CHOPPED

2 CANS CREAM OF MUSHROOM SOUP

1 CAN CHICKEN BROTH

1 PT. FRESH MUSHROOMS

⅓ C. SHERRY

Salt and pepper pheasant and brown in butter. Remove pheasant. Lightly brown onion in drippings. Add cream of mushroom soup. Thin with chicken broth. Add fresh mushrooms that have been sauteed in butter. Add Sherry. Pour over pheasant in casserole. Bake covered in 325° oven for 2½ hours. Can be done ahead and reheated. Gravy good over wild rice. Serves 8.

HINT: Place oranges in a hot oven for a few minutes before peeling. No white fiber will be left on the orange.

"FAN FARE" FRUITED CHICKEN

3 LG. CHICKEN BREASTS, 2 LBS., BONED AND SKINNED

1 CHICKEN BOUILLON CUBE

¼ TSP. GRATED ORANGE PEEL

¼ C. ORANGE JUICE

1 TBSP. CHOPPED GREEN ONION

1 TBSP. CORNSTARCH

½ C. HALVED AND SEEDED TOKAY OR SEEDLESS GREEN GRAPES

PAPRIKA

1 MED. ORANGE, SLICED

Cut chicken breasts in half lengthwise. Sprinkle with salt; arrange chicken in 10x6x1¾" baking dish. Dissolve bouillon cube in ½ C. boiling water; stir in orange peel, orange juice, chopped green onion, and dash pepper. Pour over chicken. Cover with foil; bake at 350° till tender, about 50 to 60 mins. Remove chicken to warm serving platter. Strain pan juices, reserving ¾ C. for sauce. In saucepan blend cornstarch with 2 Tbsp. cold water; stir in reserved pan juices. Cook, stirring constantly, till mixture is thick and bubbly; cook 1 min. longer. Stir in grapes; heat through. To serve, spoon sauce over chicken; sprinkle with paprika. Garnish with orange slices. Serves 6.

REFEREE'S NOTE: *At 157 calories per serving, what fans wouldn't go nuts?*

"FOREARM SHIVER" CHICKEN BATTER

2 WHOLE EGGS

JUICE OF 2 LEMONS

1 C. FLOUR

2 C. MILK

REFEREE'S NOTE: *Be a "polished passer" of your chicken platter with this Southern specialty.*

by RONALD ERHARDT

(Head Coach, New England Patriots)

Mix all ingredients into a batter. Salt and pepper chicken. Dip chicken in batter, then in flour. Fry chicken to a golden brown. Serves 6-8, depending on amount of chicken used.

NOTES FROM THE BENCH: *"This recipe is very popular in the South and a favorite among Fried Chicken Lovers everywhere."*

"LOST YARDAGE" HAWAIIAN HAM

1 LG. BONELESS HAM, FULLY COOKED AND TRIM FAT

⅓ C. PINEAPPLE JUICE

2 TBSP. SOY SAUCE

¾ TSP. GROUND GINGER

½ GARLIC CLOVE, MINCED

1 SM. CAN PINEAPPLE SLICES, JUICE PACKED

Slice ham into 4 portions. Blend pineapple juice, soy sauce, ginger, and garlic. Pour over ham in shallow container. Marinate 30 mins. turning once. Remove ham from marinade; reserve marinade. Grill over hot coals till heated through, about 2 mins. on each side. Brush often with marinade. Heat 4 pineapple slices on grill during last 2 mins. Serve pineapple atop. Serves 4.

REFEREE'S NOTE: Outrageous outdoor cookery at a mere 219 calories per serving and a wonderful way to loose a little yardage at the same time!

MINNESOTA WILD RICE AND TURKEY CASSEROLE

1 C. WILD RICE, UNCOOKED

2 C. CELERY, CHOPPED, ABOUT 4 STALKS

1 - 8 OZ. CAN CHOPPED MUSHROOMS, OR 1 LB. FRESH MUSHROOMS, CHOPPED

¼ SM. ONION, CHOPPED

4 C. DICED TURKEY CHUNKS (EASIEST TO BUY 1-2 LB. FROZEN TURKEY ROAST, DIVIDE INTO 2 PORTIONS)

¼ C. BUTTER

3 TBSP. SOY SAUCE

¾ C. WATER

1 - 10 OZ. CAN OF CREAM OF MUSHROOM SOUP

by PAT GRANT

(Bud Grant, Head Coach, Minnesota Vikings)

Cook the rice according to package directions. In large skillet, add celery, mushrooms, onion, turkey and butter. Cook, stirring constantly for about 5 mins. Combine rice, soy sauce, soup and water with turkey mixture, stirring to mix well. Pour into 2 qt. casserole or baking dish. Cover and bake at 350° for 2 hours. Serves 6-8.

REFEREE'S NOTE: Aromatic and flavorful — and so good!

Pat Grant

"FAVORED" DEVILED STEAK

1½ LBS. BEEF SIRLOIN STEAK, 1" THICK

2 TBSP. BUTTER OR MARGARINE

1 TBSP. SNIPPED PARSLEY

1 TBSP. DRY SHERRY

1 TSP. DRY MUSTARD

1 TSP. WORCESTERSHIRE SAUCE

2 TBSP. WARM BRANDY

¼ C. CATSUP

1 - 4 OZ. CAN SLICED MUSHROOMS, DRAINED

Trim excess fat from meat. Broil 3 inches from heat for 5 to 6 mins. on each side; steak will be rare. In large skillet combine butter, next 4 ingredients, ¼ tsp. salt, and dash pepper; heat till bubbly. Add steak; pour brandy over. Flame. When brandy has burned down, remove steak. Add catsup and mushrooms to skillet; mix well. Serve over steak. Serves 6.

REFEREE'S NOTE: A true eye opening course, flamed at your table, and a slimming main dish at only 215 calories per serving.

ABE'S FAVORITE LAMB CHOPS

12 LAMB CHOPS, ¼" THICK
SALT AND PEPPER TO TASTE
OREGANO
LEMON JUICE

by ABE GIBRON
(Assistant Head Coach, Tampa Bay Buccaneers)

Have your butcher cut chops ¼" thick. Salt, pepper and add generous sprinkle of oregano to each chop. Put under a hot broiler and sear quickly on both sides. As soon as they come out of the broiler, put on a hot serving platter and add fresh lemon juice. Serves 4.

REFEREE'S NOTE: Abe's favorite — "fair call."

Abe Gibron

PERNICANO'S PORK CHOPS

CENTER CUT PORK CHOPS, TRIMMED
SALT
PEPPER
GARLIC CLOVES, CHOPPED

by GEORGE PERNICANO
(Part Owner, San Diego Chargers)

Sprinkle salt and pepper on pork chops to taste, then rub with garlic. Broil or barbecue chops, about 10 mins. per side. Remove chops to a plate and bake in a 500° oven for 5 mins. more.

REFEREE'S NOTE: Sounds simple? We bet it'll take only one attempt for a successful completion.

George Pernicano

STIR-FRIED PORK WITH ALMONDS

1 LB. LEAN BONELESS PORK SHOULDER

2 TBSP. CORNSTARCH

2 TBSP. SOY SAUCE

⅛ TSP. GARLIC POWDER

4 TBSP. SALAD OIL

¾ C. WHOLE BLANCHED ALMONDS

1 LG. ONION, SLICED ½" THICK, THEN HALVED

1 - 8 OZ. CAN SLICED WATER CHESTNUTS, DRAINED

1 - 6 OZ. PKG. FROZEN SNOW PEAS, THAWED, or 1 - 9 OZ. FROZEN CUT GREEN BEANS

1 C. CHICKEN BROTH

½ TSP. BEAU MONDE SEASONING

3 C. HOT COOKED RICE

In a small bowl, combine pork and marinade made of cornstarch, soy sauce, and garlic powder. Let stand at room temperature 20 to 30 mins., stirring occasionally. Heat 1 Tbsp. oil in large skillet. Add almonds and brown on medium heat, stirring constantly, about 2 mins. Remove almonds and reserve. Heat remaining 3 Tbsp. of oil in same skillet. Add pork marinade and onions. Fry, stirring constantly, over medium-high heat 5 mins. or until pork is cooked. Stir in almonds, water chestnuts, snow peas, chicken broth, and Beau Monde. Cook, stirring constantly, until liquid is thickened. Serve with rice. Makes 4 to 8 servings.

"GRID IRON" PORK CHOPS

PORK CHOPS, CENTER CUT,
1" THICK AT LEAST
SEASONED SALT
2-3 TBSP. WHITE WINE
SEASONED SALT: 2 TBSP. SALT
2 TBSP. SUGAR
2 TBSP. M.S.G.
1 TBSP. BLACK PEPPER
1 TBSP. DRY LEMON POWDER
1 TBSP. PAPRIKA (OPTIONAL)

by JOHN THOMPSON
(General Manager, Seattle Seahawks)

Sprinkle both sides of chops liberally with seasoned salt mix. Grill over hot coals until seared and brown on both sides. Pour wine in bottom of frying pan which can be placed without damage over the barbecue grill. If barbecue cannot be covered, use lid or foil on frying pan and steam for about 25-30 mins.

NOTES FROM THE BENCH: *"Eastern Washington University, training camp of the Seahawks, and Governor Dixie Ray considered this tasty recipe good enough to institute a Master Chef Award, which isn't bad for a left-hander, is it?"*

John Thompson

KANSAS CITY LONDON BROIL

2 OR 3 LB. LONDON BROIL, FLANK STEAK
WISHBONE SALAD DRESSING

REFEREE'S NOTE: *Serve with a veteran's confidence when you need a sure play.*

by JAN STENERUD
(#3, PK, Kansas City Chiefs)

Cover and marinate London Broil in Wishbone Salad Dressing for 12 hours. Serves 6.

NOTES FROM THE BENCH: *"It is the best steak in the world!"*

Jan Stenerud

PURPLE PEOPLE EATERS PEPPERROAST

BONELESS SIRLOIN TIP ROAST OR TOP ROUND, ½ LB. PER PERSON
½ C. COARSE BLACK PEPPER
½ TSP. CARDAMOM SEED
1 TSP. CATSUP
½ TSP. GARLIC POWDER
1 TSP. PAPRIKA
1 C. SOY SAUCE
¾ C. VINEGAR

Combine black pepper and Cardamom seed and place the mixture with the roast in a plastic bag. Rub the seasoning thoroughly on the roast and let it sit for 30 mins. The use of a plastic bag keeps your hands clean. In a shallow baking dish, mix catsup, garlic powder, paprika, soy sauce, and vinegar. Pour the ingredients over the roast and let it marinate overnight in the refrigerator, turning over the roast as many times as possible. Wrap the roast in aluminum foil and roast for 2 hours (5 lb. roast would be medium rare). Strain the left over juice and pour over the roast for a delicious gravy. Slice thin and keep well-covered while transporting to your tailgate.

REFEREE'S NOTE: *Contributed by the Vikings' favorite butcher, Jim Biglow, who knows the art of tailgate cooking.*

#1 FAN PORK CHOPS SUPREME

6 PORK CHOPS

1 ENVELOPE DRIED ONION SOUP MIX

⅔ C. EVAPORATED MILK

4 OZ. CAN MUSHROOM PIECES

2-3 C. COOKED RICE

¼ C. FLOUR

1 TBSP. PARSLEY FLAKES

NOTES FROM THE BENCH: "I'm not sure if I like this recipe because it's good or because the Lady who makes it for me is so cute!"

by CHARLIE GETTY

(#77, G-T, Kansas City Chiefs)

Brown pork chops. Salt and pepper to taste. Drain off drippings. Mix dry onion soup mix with enough hot water to almost cover pork chops. Pour over pork chops. Cover and cook over low heat till tender. Stir mushrooms into flour. Take skillet off heat. Remove chops and keep warm. Stir the flour mixture, parsley flakes and evaporated milk into liquid in skillet. Stir over low heat till steaming. Do not boil. Dip chops in gravy to cover with sauce. Serve over rice. Serves 4-6.

"SUPERBOWL" SPAGHETTI WITH COGNAC AND SOUR CREAM SAUCE

2 TBSP. OLIVE OIL

¼ C. BUTTER

1 SM. ONION, CHOPPED

2 CLOVES GARLIC, FINELY CHOPPED

1 LB. GROUND ROUND OR SIRLOIN STEAK

SALT AND FRESHLY GROUND PEPPER TO TASTE

1 - 2 LB. 3 OZ. CAN TOMATOES WITH TOMATO PASTE (OR USE 5 CUPS CANNED TOMATOES AND 3 TBSP. TOMATO PASTE)

¾ CAN FRESH OR CANNED BEEF BROTH

1 HOT, DRIED RED PEPPER, OPTIONAL

2 TBSP. PARSLEY, FINELY CHOPPED

1 LB. SPAGHETTINI, SPAGHETTI OR VERMICELLI

2 TBSP. COGNAC

4 to 8 TBSP. SOUR CREAM

¾ C. GRATED PARMESAN CHEESE

Heat the oil and butter in a casserole and when it is hot, add the onion and garlic, stirring. Cook until onion is wilted and starts to brown and add the meat, salt and pepper. Cook, stirring and breaking up lumps in the meat with the side of a large kitchen spoon. When there are no more lumps and the meat has lost its raw color, add tomatoes, broth, red pepper and parsley. Cook, stirring occasionally, 45 mins. to an hour or until sauce is thickened. Meanwhile, cook the pasta to the desired degree of doneness. Add the Cognac to the spaghetti sauce and bring to a boil. Serve the spaghetti piping hot with the sauce on the side or toss the spaghetti with the sauce and serve. Let each person help himself or herself to the sour cream and grated cheese. Serves 4.

REFEREE'S NOTE: A unique balance of ingredients and surely a Superbowl super dish.

"LINE OF SCRIMMAGE" CHOP SUEY

2½ LBS. CHOP SUEY MEAT (PORK, BEEF, AND VEAL) CUBED

½ TSP. SALT

¼ TSP. PEPPER

2½ TSP. SOY SAUCE

1 MED. ONION, CHOPPED

1½ C. CELERY, DICED

1 - 28 OZ. CAN CHOP SUEY VEGETABLES

1 - 16 OZ. CAN BEAN SPROUTS

2 - 10 OZ. CANS CREAM OF MUSHROOM SOUP

1 - 8 OZ. CAN MUSHROOMS

2 C. WATER

2 C. RICE

2 - 3 OZ. CANS CHOW MEIN NOODLES

"CENTER SNAP" SCALLOPS

1 LB. SCALLOPS

FLOUR

BUTTER

½ C. ONIONS

¼ C. GREEN PEPPER, CHOPPED

1 LB. MUSHROOMS

3-4 TOMATO WEDGES

"CURL PATTERN" SHRIMP

LARGE BENGLADESH SHRIMP OR PRAWNS IN THEIR SHELL

LEMON JUICE

CELERY SALT

BLACK PEPPER

MELTED BUTTER

by BRAD VANPELT
(#10, LB, New York Giants)

Brown meat. Add salt, pepper, onion and celery — continue browning to transparent stage of onion and celery. Add Chop Suey vegetables, bean sprouts, soup, mushrooms and water. Cook at medium heat for 30 mins. Reduce heat to simmer for additional 1½ hours, stirring occasionally adding water if necessary. Prepare rice as directed on package. Serve Chop Suey over rice and chow mein noodles. Note: Salt, pepper and soy sauce may be added depending on individual taste. Also, Chop Suey may be thickened if desired. Serves 8-10.

NOTES FROM THE BENCH: "There isn't one of my birthdays that goes by without these dinners being part of my day. And no one can cook them better than Dear Ol' Mom!"

Brad VanPelt

by DAREN BROCK
(Pete Brock, #58, C, New England Patriots)

Coat scallops lightly with flour and saute in butter 4-5 mins. until golden. Add onions, salt to taste, green pepper and cook 1 min. Add mushrooms and cook 3-4 mins. or until mushrooms are done. Add fresh tomato wedges at very end and cook about 2 mins.

REFEREE'S NOTE: This sumptuous seafood is a snap!

by RAY MALAVASI
(Head Coach, Los Angeles Rams)

Split shrimp shells. Marinate shrimp in lemon juice, celery salt, pepper to taste for 6-8 hours. Barbecue until shrimp turn bright red. Serve with melted butter.

REFEREE'S NOTE: Outdoor chefs — take this from your playbook for a winning approach.

"DOWN AND OUT" CHEESE FONDUE

¾ LB. NATURAL SWISS CHEESE, JULIENNE STRIPS, ABOUT 3 C.

1 TBSP. FLOUR

1 GARLIC CLOVE, HALVED

1¼ C. SAUTERNE

DASH FRESHLY GROUND PEPPER

DASH NUTMEG

3 TBSP. DRY SHERRY

FRENCH BREAD OR HARD ROLLS, TORN OR CUT IN BITE-SIZE PIECES, EACH WITH AT LEAST ONE SIDE OF CRUST

Toss cheese with flour to coat. Rub inside of fondue pot vigorously with cut surface of garlic. Pour in Sauterne and warm just till air bubbles start to rise. Don't cover, do not boil. Stir all the time from now on; add a handful of cheese strips. Wait till cheese has melted before tossing in another handful. After all the cheese has been blended in, and mixture is gently bubbling, stir in seasonings and Sherry. Now invite guests to dunk — down and out. Each spears a cube of bread on a long-handled fork and dips into the melted cheese. If fondue becomes too thick, pour in a little warmed Sauterne. Serves 5 to 6.

REFEREE'S NOTE: For a cheese appreciation night.

"WEIGH IN" TORSK

1 LB. TORSK, DEFROSTED

½ C. WHITE WINE

¼ C. WATER

¼ TBSP. TARRAGON

2 SLICES LEMON

1 MED. ONION, SLICED

SALT AND PEPPER

¼ LB. FRESH MUSHROOMS, SLICED

1 SLICE ONION, DICED

¼ C. WHITE WINE

by JERRY REICHOW
(Coordinator of Football Operations, Minnesota Vikings)

Poach torsk in white wine, water and tarragon. Place onion and lemon on top of fish, salt and pepper and microwave in shallow, covered dish for 10 mins. Or bake covered in a 350° oven for 25 mins. Drain fish thoroughly on paper towel. Meanwhile, saute mushrooms and onion (2 Tbsp.) using a spray oil in pan instead of butter. Add ¼ C. white wine, a little more tarragon and serve immediately. Serves 2-3.

REFEREE'S NOTE: For a third and short situation, try this dish — it has curative powers at only 147 calories per serving.

"HOOK PATTERN" PIKE

3 LBS. WALLEYED PIKE FILLETS, OR ANY WHITEFISH

1 C. SOUR CREAM

¼ C. BUTTER OR MARGARINE, MELTED

½ C. PARMESAN CHEESE

½ TSP. SALT

½ TSP. PEPPER

PARSLEY, CHOPPED

by PAT GRANT
(Bud Grant, Head Coach, Minnesota Vikings)

Wipe pike fillets off with clean, damp cloth, pat dry and place in lightly greased, shallow baking pan. Combine next 5 ingredients and spread over fillets in pan. Bake at 350° for 30 mins., remove from oven and sprinkle with chopped parsley. Serve immediately or cover with lid or aluminum foil and take to game (if the distance to the stadium is 30 mins. or so). Serves 5.

REFEREE'S NOTE: Coach Grant has a winning strategy with this Minnesota walleye dish.

JOHN ZOOK'S LOCKER ROOM FISH FRY

FILLET OF BASS OR OTHER FRESHWATER FISH

WATER

WHITE CORN MEAL

FLOUR

SALT

PEPPER

GARLIC POWDER

BUTTER

by JOHN ZOOK
(#63, DE, St. Louis Cardinals)

The quantity of batter made varies with the number of fish fillets. To make the batter use approximately equal parts corn meal and flour. Add salt, pepper and garlic salt to taste. Dip fillets in water and then in batter. Fry fillets in butter until done, about 7 mins. per side. If using electric skillet, set at 300°.

REFEREE'S NOTE: Ask any St. Louis Cardinal player and he'll tell you the last time John cooked for the team it took him 4 hours and 55 pounds of bass fillets.

John Zook

SHRIMP SAUTE DELLA CASA

8 SHRIMPS, EXTRA-JUMBO SIZE

1 SHALLOT, FINELY CHOPPED

⅛ LB. BUTTER

⅓ C. WHITE WINE, FAIRLY DRY

⅓ C. WHIPPING CREAM

SALT, PEPPER

FRESH LEMON JUICE

by CHARLOTTE JOHNSON
(Andy Johnson, #32, RB, New England Patriots)

Peel and devein shrimp. Flour shrimp lightly and saute in butter for 2-3 mins. Add shallots, saute 1 min. more. Remove shrimp and reduce sauce with white wine until it resembles thick juice. Add cream and reduce once more to a thick sauce. Replace shrimp in pan. Add salt and pepper and lemon juice. Cook 1-2 mins. under broiler to insure tenderness in shrimp. Serve immediately with a broiled tomato or broccoli. Serves 1.

REFEREE'S NOTE: This dish holds the culinary promise that your guests will be "running back" for more.

SEA BASS FRANCESI

SEA BASS FILLETS

SALT

PEPPER

FLOUR

1-2 EGGS, BEATEN

OLIVE OIL

MUSHROOMS, SLICED

BUTTER

DRY WHITE WINE

GARLIC, CHOPPED

DASH LEMON JUICE

by GEORGE PERNICANO
(Part-owner, San Diego Chargers)

Sprinkle fillets with salt and pepper. Coat with flour, then dip in egg. Pan fry fillets in a small amount of olive oil. Saute mushrooms in butter with a little wine, garlic, and lemon juice. Spoon mushrooms over fish and serve.

REFEREE'S NOTE: Garlic — snipped in the bud!

"CROSSING PATTERN" LASAGNA

1 -8 OZ. PKG. LASAGNA NOODLES

1¾ LB. GROUND BEEF

2 TBSP. SALAD OIL, OPTIONAL

1 QT. CANNED TOMATOES

½ TSP. GARLIC SALT

3 TBSP. FLOUR

¼ C. ONION, MINCED

1½ TSP. SALT

¼ TSP. PEPPER

8 OZ. COTTAGE CHEESE

1½ TSP. OREGANO

1 SM. CAN TOMATO SAUCE OR PASTE

½ LB. MOZZARELLA CHEESE, GRATED OR THINLY SLICED

½ C. PARMESAN CHEESE

by ROBBI GROGAN
(Steve Grogan, #14, QB, New England Patriots)

Cook and drain noodles. Brown beef in oil (optional) and add garlic salt. Mix ¼ C. of the canned tomato juice with the flour and add to beef. Add remaining tomatoes and juice, onion, salt, pepper and oregano. Simmer 10-15 mins. and pour off excess grease. Grease a 7x11" or 9x10" dish. Layer beef, noodles, cheese and cottage cheese. End with last of beef. Pour on top tomato sauce and add Parmesan cheese. Bake 375° for 20-25 mins. Reduce to 350° for 50-60 mins. Allow to stand for 10 mins. before cutting.

SIDELINE STRATEGIST'S LASAGNA

1 BOX LASAGNA NOODLES

1 LB. RICOTTA CHEESE

1 LB. PRIME GROUND BEEF

1 LB. GROUND VEAL

1½ LBS. MOZZARELLA CHEESE

1 LB. PARMESAN AND ROMANO CHEESE, GRATED AND MIXED

1 LB. ITALIAN SAUSAGE

3 EGGS

OLIVE OIL

HOMEMADE OR BOTTLED ITALIAN SPAGHETTI SAUCE

1 ONION, DICED

4 TBSP. PARSLEY

by RAY MALAVASI
(Head Coach, Los Angeles Rams)

Make meat mixture: Mix the eggs, salt and pepper, ground beef and ground veal together. Brown in olive oil with diced onions and parsley. Set aside. Fry sausage until ¾ cooked and slice into small pieces. Set aside. Boil noodles until tender and drain. Add cold water immediately. Set aside. Cover bottom of a 9x13" casserole dish with a layer of noodles. Add ricotta cheese evenly to cover noodles. Spoon over meat mixture evenly. Cover with a thin layer of sauce. Sprinkle grated cheeses evenly over the sauce. Top with a thin layer of mozzarella slices. Spread with another thin layer of sauce. Sprinkle more grated cheese. Repeat 3 or 4 layers. Bake in a 400° oven for 35 mins. Allow to cool 10-15 mins. before serving.

REFEREE'S NOTE: *You'll have the home field advantage serving the Coach's lasagna!*

"SCORED" HAM
WITH CHERRY SAUCE

4-5 LB. HAM

1 - 10 OZ. JAR APPLE JELLY

1 TBSP. PREPARED MUSTARD

⅓ C. PINEAPPLE JUICE

⅛ C. MADEIRA WINE

1 - 21 OZ. CAN CHERRY PIE FILLING

½ C. LIGHT RAISINS

Place ham, fat side up, on rack in shallow pan; bake in 325° oven for time indicated. One-half hour before done, take ham from oven and score top. Combine jelly, mustard, juice and wine; boil, then simmer 3 mins. Pour ⅓ mixture on ham and return to oven. Spoon on rest of mixture at 2 to 10 min. intervals. Remove ham and add glaze in pan to pie filling and raisins. Boil. Spoon some over ham and serve rest separately as a sauce. Serves 10-12.

UNREAL VEAL

2 LBS. CALF ROUND STEAK OR SCALLOPS CUT FROM BEEF

EYE OF ROUND

½ C. FLOUR

SALT AND PEPPER

2 TBSP. SWEET PAPRIKA

4 TBSP. OLIVE OIL

1 - 4 OZ. CAN SLICED MUSHROOMS

1 BEEF BOUILLON CUBE

1 - 8 OZ. CAN TOMATO SAUCE

¼ C. GREEN PEPPER, CHOPPED

PARMESAN CHEESE

by JOHN OWENS

(Sports Editor, Seattle Post-Intelligencer)

Dust the meat in a mixture of the flour, salt, pepper and paprika. Heat 3 Tbsp. olive oil in the skillet and brown the meat on both sides, removing to a large flat oven dish as you finish each piece. Separate the mushrooms from the liquid and add enough water to the mushroom juice to make one cup. Bring to a boil, plunk in the bouillon cube and pour over the "veal." Bake 30 mins. in a 350° oven. While it's cooking, combine the mushrooms, tomato sauce and chopped green pepper. At the end of 30 mins., pour this sauce over the veal and return to the oven for another 15 mins. Cook the noodles in salted water that also contains 1 Tbsp. of olive oil. Drain the noodles, "plunk" them on the platter, add the scallops, "smear" the sauce over everything, sprinkle generously with Parmesan cheese, and serve with a side dish of broccoli. Serves 4 to 6.

REFEREE'S NOTE: *We drop back and pass this one on to you as is — it's unreal.*

THE EXTRA EFFORT

GRAPES A LA RASHAD

6 C. STEMMED SEEDLESS GRAPES

¾ C. BROWN SUGAR

1 PT. SOUR CREAM

REFEREE'S NOTE: When time is running out and dessert is fourth down, don't punt. This recipe is Ahmad's answer to a special dessert in a hurry.

by AHMAD RASHAD

(#28, WR, Minnesota Vikings)

Wash grapes; drain well. Spread in flat shallow dish (or individual serving dishes) and sprinkle with brown sugar. Top this with sour cream. Refrigerate for 1 hour or more. Serves 6. Note: Brown sugar may be sprinkled on top of sour cream.

HALF TIME COOKIES

1 C. OIL

½ C. SUGAR

½ C. BROWN SUGAR

1 TBSP. WATER

2 EGG YOLKS

1 TSP. VANILLA

2 C. FLOUR

¼ TSP. BAKING SODA

½ TSP. BAKING POWDER

1 LG. PKG. CHOCOLATE CHIPS

2 EGG WHITES

1 C. BROWN SUGAR

by OTTO GRAHAM

(Hall of Fame, Former Cleveland Browns QB)

Mix well. Spread out onto an ungreased 9x12″ pan. Sprinkle with chocolate chips. Top with 2 egg whites beaten stiff with 1 C. brown sugar. Bake 20-25 mins. at 350°.

NOTES FROM THE BENCH: "These cookies are especially good when the grandchildren are visiting."

BRING FROM HOME BROWNIES

1 C. BUTTER OR MARGARINE

4 SQUARES UNSWEETENED CHOCOLATE

2 C. SUGAR

4 EGGS

2 TSP. VANILLA

1½ C. ALL-PURPOSE FLOUR, SIFTED

¼ C. NUTS, CHOPPED (OPTIONAL)

¼ C. POWDERED SUGAR

by PAT GRANT

(Bud Grant, Head Coach, Minnesota Vikings)

In large saucepan, melt butter and chocolate over low heat. Remove from heat and stir in sugar. Cool slightly. Add eggs, one at a time, blending thoroughly after each addition. Add vanilla, blend well. Slowly stir in flour and nuts, a little at a time to avoid lumping. Mix well. Spread brownie mixture evenly in lightly greased 9x13″ pan. Bake at 350° for 30 mins. Do not overbake. Allow to cool slightly and sprinkle the brownies with powdered sugar.

REFEREE'S NOTE: Ideal for tailgating and oh-so good!

CHERRY STARR'S COCONUT PECAN CAKE

½ C. MARGARINE

½ C. SHORTENING

5 EGGS, SEPARATED

1 TSP. VANILLA

2 C. SIFTED ALL-PURPOSE FLOUR

1 TSP. SODA

½ TSP. SALT

1 C. BUTTERMILK

1 - 3½ OZ. CAN FLAKED COCONUT

1 C. PECANS, CHOPPED

"NO FUMBLE" FUDGE SAUCE

1 - 14½ OZ. CAN EVAPORATED MILK

2 C. SUGAR

4 SQUARES, 1 OZ. EACH, UNSWEETENED CHOCOLATE

1 TSP. VANILLA

½ TSP. SALT

¼ C. BUTTER

PRIME TIME PUMPKIN PIE

1½ C. PUMPKIN

¾ C. SUGAR

½ TSP. SALT

½ TBSP. GINGER

¼-½ TBSP. NUTMEG

¼-½ TBSP. CLOVES

1 TBSP. CINNAMON

3 EGGS, SLIGHTLY BEATEN

1 - 6 OZ. CAN EVAPORATED MILK

1 C. MILK

by CHERRY STARR
(Bart Starr, General Manager and Head Coach, Green Bay Packers)

Cream margarine and shortening until light and fluffy. Add 1½ C. sugar gradually; beat again until light and fluffy. Add egg yolks and vanilla; beat thoroughly. Add flour sifted with soda and salt in thirds alternately with buttermilk, beating until smooth after each addition. Turn batter into a 3 qt. mixing bowl. Beat egg whites until stiff but not dry; beat remaining ½ C. sugar in gradually. Fold egg whites into batter gently but thoroughly. Fold in coconut and pecans. Spread batter in 3 greased, wax paper-lined, and again greased 9″ cake pans. Bake at 375° for about 25 mins. or until brown. Fill and frost as you wish. We use a boiled icing with additional coconut. Whipped cream also would be good. Serves 12.

NOTES FROM THE BENCH: *"Bart doesn't eat many desserts but he loves this special cake."*

Cherry Starr

by BILL KOLLAR
(#77, DE-DT, Tampa Bay Buccaneers)

In saucepan, heat milk and sugar to boiling, stirring constantly. Boil and stir one min. Reduce heat. Stir in chocolate till smooth. Remove from heat and stir in butter, vanilla and salt. Makes 3 C.

REFEREE'S NOTE: *Assuming you've done a couple of laps before dessert, enjoy!*

Bill Kollar

by FRAN TARKENTON
(Sportscaster, ABC, Former Minnesota Vikings QB)

Combine pumpkin, sugar and spices. Blend. Add eggs and milk; mix thoroughly. Pour into 9″ pastry lined pie pan. Bake at 450° for 10 mins., reduce to 325° and bake 50 mins. longer.

NOTES FROM THE BENCH: *"I am a great lover of desserts. This is among the best."*

Fran Tarkenton

"ROLL OUT" ANGEL WINGS

1 C. QUICK OATMEAL
1 C. SUGAR
⅔ C. BUTTER, MELTED
¼ C. WHIPPING CREAM
¼ C. WHITE CORN SYRUP
1 C. FLOUR LESS 1 TBSP.
½ TSP. BAKING POWDER
1 TSP. VANILLA

by JACK CHRISTIANSEN
(Hall of Fame, Detroit Lions, DS)

Put oatmeal, sugar, butter, whipping cream and corn syrup in a bowl, mix together. Add flour, baking powder and stir. Add vanilla. Drop by teaspoons onto greased cookie sheet. Bake 7-9 mins. at 375°. Remove from oven, let stand about 1 min. Remove from cookie sheet and place on rolling pin or round object and allow to cool.

REFEREE'S NOTE: Clever maneuvering will insure success with these delicacies originating from Borlange, Sweden.

"TRIPLE TEAMING" RAW APPLE CAKE

STEP ONE:
4 C. APPLES, SLICED
2 EGGS

STEP TWO:
½ C. OIL
2 C. SUGAR

STEP THREE:
2 C. FLOUR
2 TSP. BAKING SODA
½ TSP. SALT
2 TSP. CINNAMON

STEP FOUR:
1½ C. DATES, PITTED AND CUT UP
1 C. NUTS, CHOPPED

STEP FIVE:
½ C. SUGAR
⅓ C. FLOUR
1 TBSP. CINNAMON
½ C. BUTTER

by PETER CRONAN
(#57, LB, Seattle Seahawks)

Break eggs over sliced apples and stir.

Mix and stir into above mixture.

Combine and add to above mixture.

Combine and add to above mixture. Pour into greased 9x13" pan.

Combine and sprinkle over cake. Bake at 350° 60 mins. or until done.

REFEREE'S NOTE: End your meal with this "spectacular performance."

GEORGIA CAKE

DUNCAN HINES BUTTER RECIPE
CAKE MIX

FROSTING:

2 C. SUGAR

¼ C. COCOA

⅔ C. MILK

½ C. SOLID SHORTENING

3 LG. MARSHMALLOWS, CUT UP

BENCH WARMER COOKIES

2 EGG WHITES

⅔ C. SUGAR

PINCH OF SALT

6 OZ. PKG. CHOCOLATE CHIPS

1 C. PECANS

1 TSP. VANILLA

ROMAN'S NATURAL
ENERGY CAKE

½ C. BUTTER

1-1½ C. HONEY (DEPENDING ON HOW
SWEET YOU WANT IT)

2 EGGS

1½ MED. (9 OZ.) CANS CRUSHED
PINEAPPLE, IN OWN JUICE

1 TBSP. LEMON JUICE

½ TSP. SALT

1 TSP. BAKING SODA

1 TSP. VANILLA

2-3 C. WHOLE WHEAT FLOUR

1 C. RAISINS

1 C. WALNUTS

by RICH SAUL

(#61, C, Los Angeles Rams)

Mix cake according to directions except bake in 8″ layer
pans so that batter makes 6 layers. Bake 2 layers at a
time at 400° for 5-7 mins. Remove from pans and cool.
Frost tort-like with chocolate frosting. Frosting: Mix all
ingredients in sauce pan and allow to boil 3 mins.
Frosting will be thin but will harden on cooked cake.

NOTES FROM THE BENCH: *"Jack Youngblood and I
have eaten one of these cakes in one sitting!"*

by PAT MINER

(Tom Miner, Scout, Cleveland Browns)

Beat egg whites stiff, add sugar and salt. Fold in
chocolate chips, pecans and vanilla. Line a cookie sheet
with foil, drop by spoonfuls on cookie sheet. Put in a
preheated 350° oven. Then, turn off oven and leave
cookies in overnight with door closed. Makes 30 cookies.

REFEREE'S NOTE: *What a surprise for any scout or
food snoop to find these in the oven, warming overnight!*

by ROMAN GABRIEL

(Former Los Angeles Rams & Philadelphia Eagles QB)

Melt butter and honey in skillet. Beat, by hand, 2 eggs in
mixing bowl. Add butter and honey. Beat in pineapple
and its juice. Add lemon juice, salt, soda and vanilla. Mix
in wheat flour until you get a good consistency. Add
raisins and walnuts. Pour into well-oiled cake pan and
bake at 350° for 40-60 mins. Top of cake should be firm.
Serves 10-12. Note: When making this cake, use
uncooked, unfiltered honey, and sea salt.

NOTES FROM THE BENCH: *"This is great for an energy
boost for workouts or as a snack between meals. For
people interested in gaining weight, a few of these cakes
for dessert will surely help."*

"M.V.P." — MOST VALUABLE PINEAPPLE DESSERT

1¼ C. GRAHAM CRACKER CRUMBS (16)

2 TBSP. GRANULATED SUGAR

¼ C. BUTTER OR MARGARINE, MELTED

½ C. BUTTER OR MARGARINE, SOFTENED

1 C. CONFECTIONER'S SUGAR

1 EGG

1 C. WHIPPING CREAM

1 - 1 LB. 4 OZ. CAN CRUSHED PINEAPPLE

SWEETENED WHIPPED CREAM

MARASCHINO CHERRIES

by BETSY HASSELBECK
(Don Hasselbeck, #80, TE, New England Patriots)

Mix graham cracker crumbs, granulated sugar and melted butter. Press half the crumb mixture evenly in bottom of pan, 8x8x2". Beat together ½ C. butter, confectioner's sugar and egg until mixture is light and fluffy. Spread carefully and evenly over crumbs in pan. In chilled bowl, beat cream until stiff. If using dessert topping, prepare as on package directions. Fold in well drained pineapple. Spread over butter mixture. Sprinkle with remaining graham cracker crumbs. Cover. Chill 12 hours. Cut into squares and serve with whipped cream and maraschino cherries.

REFEREE'S NOTE: The mainstay of old-fashioned refrigerator desserts.

"TWO MINUTE WARNING" FUDGE

3 C. SUGAR

3 HEAPING TBSP. COCOA

½ C. CREAM

3 TBSP. KARO SYRUP

¼ C. BUTTER

1 TSP. VANILLA

PECAN HALVES

by BILL BROWN
(Former Minnesota Vikings FB)

Cook first 5 ingredients until soft ball stage, 238°. Add butter and vanilla. Cool to 110° until fudge loses shine. Form into balls with buttered hands. Top with pecan half.

REFEREE'S NOTE: To satisfy the wanton need to devour something excessively sinful.

GRANDSTAND POUND CAKE

2 C. BUTTER, NOT MARGARINE

2 C. SUGAR

2 TSP. VANILLA

½ TSP. ALMOND EXTRACT OR 1 TSP. LEMON EXTRACT

8 LG. EGGS, SEPARATED

3 C. ALL-PURPOSE FLOUR

1 TSP. BAKING POWDER

½ TSP. SALT

NOTES FROM THE BENCH: Green Bay Safety Howard Sampson says, "This is one of the finest pound cake recipes." It comes from his Mother's Mother.

by HOWARD SAMPSON
(#36, S, Green Bay Packers)

Cream butter until light and fluffy; gradually adding sugar, beating well after each addition of sugar. Blend in flour. Beat egg yolks until thick, add lemon or almond extract. Stir into butter mixture. Sift flour, baking powder and salt together. Add flour to butter mixture, one third at a time. Stir well after each portion. Beat egg whites until fluffy but not dry. Pour into batter then blend. Pour mixture into a buttered and lightly floured 10" tube pan. Bake at 350° for 30 mins., reduce heat to 300° and cook until done, about 1 hour and 15 mins. Cool for 10 mins. before serving.

Howard E. Sampson

PUNT, PASS, KICK AND CHEWY CARAMELS

2 C. SUGAR

1 C. WHITE SYRUP

1 PT. HEAVY CREAM

½ C. BUTTER

PINCH OF SALT

1½ TSP. VANILLA

NUTS, CHOPPED (OPTIONAL)

NOTES FROM THE BENCH: "These are super caramels that my sister makes at Christmas time. She knows I have a sweet tooth."

RASPBERRY RAINBOW CAKE

1 WHITE CAKE MIX

1 - 3 OZ. PKG. RASPBERRY JELLO

2 TBSP. FLOUR

4 EGGS

1 C. WATER

½ C. OIL

½ JAR RASPBERRY PRESERVES

1-2 PKGS. DREAM WHIP

½-1 C. MILK

"WEAKSIDE" CANOLI

1 LB. RICOTTA CHEESE

½ C. POWDERED SUGAR

½ TSP. VANILLA

1 HERSHEY BAR WITH ALMONDS, CHOPPED

OR CANDIED FRUIT, CHOPPED

OR PISTACHIO NUTS, CHOPPED

CANOLI SHELLS (PASTRY SHELLS)

by BILL BROWN
(Former Minnesota Vikings FB)

Mix sugar, syrup, salt and ½ of cream. Cook till light brown (soft ball stage, 238°). Slowly add remaining cream. Cook till light brown again. Remove from heat, add butter. When melted, cook to 248°, or as hard as you wish when tested in cold water. Add vanilla. Pour into buttered 7x12" pan. You may add chopped nuts to the bottom of the pan.

by CHARLIE GETTY
(#77, G-T, Kansas City Chiefs)

Combine cake mix, jello, flour, eggs and water. Mix well. Add oil. Beat 2 mins. Pour into 2 greased and floured round cake pans, 9" or 8". Bake 350° for 30-35 mins. Cool cake. Spread ½ of the preserves between layers. Frost with whipped cream. Decorate with remaining preserves.

by GEORGE PERNICANO
(Part owner, San Diego Chargers)

Whip ricotta cheese at high speed until smooth, 4 mins. Add sugar and beat another 4 mins. While beating add vanilla. Chop Hershey bar and fold most of it into the cheese mixture with a spoon. Stuff canoli shells with cheese mixture. Sprinkle the remaining chocolate on the open ends and lightly dust tops of shells with powdered sugar. Note: As canoli shells (pastry) are hard to make and get just right, buy them already made from an Italian bakery or delicatessen.

REFEREE'S NOTE: Stimulate and refresh even the most wilted appetites with this ethnic edible.

"THE POINT AFTER" ANGEL CAKE

1 PKG. DUNCAN HINES ANGEL CAKE MIX

2 SM. CARTONS OF WHIPPING CREAM, WHIPPED THICK AND STIFF

1 C. SOUR CREAM

1 C. SIFTED POWDERED SUGAR

1 TSP. VANILLA

1 - 10 OZ. CARTON FROZEN RASPBERRIES OR STRAWBERRIES, THAWED AND WELL DRAINED

by MAXINE FINKS
(Jim Finks, General Manager, Chicago Bears)

Bake cake according to package directions. Cool. Cut in half. Fold sour cream gently into whipped cream. Fold in sifted powdered sugar. Add vanilla. Beat gently, just enough to mix ingredients. Fold in well drained berries. Spread between layers and on top. Serves 10-12.

REFEREE'S NOTE: *Score your last point of the meal with this sweet treat.*

"STATUE OF LIBERTY" APPLE PIE

6 LG. APPLES

½-⅔ C. SUGAR

½ TSP. CINNAMON

½ TSP. NUTMEG

2 TSP. FLOUR

1 UNBAKED PIE CRUST

½ C. BUTTER OR MARGARINE

½ C. BROWN SUGAR

1 C. FLOUR

by BOB JOHNSON
(Former Cincinnati Bengals, C)

Slice apples and mix with sugar, cinnamon, nutmeg and flour. Pour into pie pan lined with unbaked pie crust. Cream butter and brown sugar with fork, add one cup flour. This makes a crumb mixture. Sprinkle over pie. Bake in a 450° oven for 15 mins., reduce temperature to 350° and bake until done. Serves 6-8.

NOTES FROM THE BENCH: *"If Jane made this pie every night, I would weigh 400 pounds!"*

REFEREE'S NOTE: *What could be more all-American than apple pie — and such a delicious one!*

Bob Johnson

TIPSY PARSON PUDDING

2 PKG. VANILLA PUDDING MIX

4 C. MILK

2 LAYER SPONGE CAKE OR LADY FINGERS

1 JAR STRAWBERRY OR RASPBERRY JAM

1 C. WHIPPING CREAM

½ C. SHERRY

by ANDY RUSSELL
(Former Pittsburgh Steelers LB)

Make a custard of pudding using 4 C. milk. Make a 2 layer sponge cake or use lady fingers. In a large serving bowl, make layers of cake, jam, Sherry, pudding, whipped cream. Chill and serve with spoon. Best if prepared a day ahead. The Sherry will soak in the cake and blends with the jam.

NOTES FROM THE BENCH: *"This pudding was served on holidays when the Parson came to call at Thanksgiving and Christmas — an old family tradition."*

Andy Russell

"QUICK DRAW" FRUIT COCKTAIL PIE

8 OZ. BAR PHILADELPHIA CREAM CHEESE

1 CAN EAGLE BRAND MILK

1 CAN FRUIT COCKTAIL, DRAINED

1 CAN CHUNK PINEAPPLE, CUT UP PINEAPPLES

1 - 8" GRAHAM CRACKER PIE CRUST

3 EGGS, SEPARATED

2 TBSP. LEMON JUICE

¼ TSP. CREAM OF TARTAR

6 TBSP. SUGAR

½ TSP. VANILLA

by HOWARD SAMPSON
(#36, S, Green Bay Packers)

Combine cheese, egg yolks, Eagle Brand milk and lemon juice. Continue to add the rest of the ingredients, also the fruit cocktail. Add all of this to the 8" graham cracker crust. For meringue; beat egg whites and cream of tartar till foamy. Beat in sugar, 1 Tbsp. at a time. Continue beating till stiff and glossy. Beat in vanilla. Set in oven to brown topping, oven should be preheated at 350°. Remove and put in ice box for 2 hours. Serves 8.

Howard E. Sampson

"DECEPTION" SALAD-DESSERT

1 PKG. LEMON JELLO, MIX ACCORDING TO PKG. DIRECTIONS

1 C. MINIATURE MARSHMALLOWS

1 - 15½ OZ. CAN PINEAPPLE, CRUSHED, RINSED

1 BANANA, SLICED

DRESSING:

1 C. PINEAPPLE JUICE

2 TBSP. FLOUR

1 EGG, BEATEN

½ C. SUGAR

WHIPPING CREAM

by DEBBIE FOX
(Tim Fox, #48, S, New England Patriots)

Mix jello and refrigerate until thick or partially set. Add marshmallows, pineapple (reserve juice) and banana. Refrigerate until set. Mix pineapple juice, flour and sugar. Cook until thick. Add 1 beaten egg, cook a little longer on low heat. Cool. Pour over jello. Beat whipping cream and pour over top of jello.

REFEREE'S NOTE: Especially festive at a ladies luncheon or as a dessert. It makes a winning performance when served in a crystal bowl.

HINT: Slip a piece of waxed paper over the bowl when whipping cream — poke the beater through a hole in the middle — no splatters.

CHARLIE'S CHERRIES JUBILEE

1 PT. PITTED BING CHERRIES

½ TSP. ARROWROOT

2 OZ. KIRSCH

1 QT. VANILLA ICE CREAM

Pour juice from cherries into top pan of chafing dish; place directly over flame and bring to boil. Thicken with arrowroot dissolved in small amount of juice, then add cherries. Stir until heated through. Pour Kirsch over the cherries and blaze. Pour over ice cream and serve immediately. (Can be done in fry pan on stove.)

REFEREE'S NOTE: From a fan from Chicago, currently in exile in the mountains of Mexico.

"FALSE TRAP" APPLE BETTY

2 C. SOFT BREAD CRUMBS, ABOUT 3 SLICES

1½ TSP. CINNAMON

1 TSP. LEMON PEEL, GRATED

¼ TSP. SALT

4 MED. SIZE COOKING APPLES, ABOUT 3 C. SLICED

¼ C. WATER

2 TBSP. LEMON JUICE

1½ TSP. NON-CALORIC SWEETENER

by DENNIS LICK
(#70, T, Chicago Bears)

Blend together first 4 ingredients. Wash, quarter, core, pare and cut apples into slices. Spread one third of crumb mixture (first 4 items) evenly and lightly over bottom of 1 qt. greased casserole. Cover with ½ of apples. Repeat. Top with remaining crumb mixture. Blend last 3 ingredients together. Drizzle over top of mixture. Bake at 375° 25-30 mins. or until apples are tender when pierced with a fork. Serve hot or cold. Serves 6.

REFEREE'S NOTE: Only 84 calories per serving.

Dennis Lick

CHOCOLATE DECADENCE

1 LB. BITTERSWEET CHOCOLATE, IF AVAILABLE, OTHERWISE GERMAN SWEET CHOCOLATE

5 OZ. SWEET BUTTER

1 TBSP. SUGAR

1 TBSP. FLOUR

4 EGGS

WHIPPED CREAM

RASPBERRY SAUCE, PUREED

by RON MIX
(Hall of Fame, San Diego Chargers OT)

Melt chocolate and set aside. Heat eggs and sugar in pan until sugar is dissolved and mixture is lukewarm. Do not over cook. Remove egg mixture from heat and whip until it has quadrupled in volume. Fold in flour. Stir ¼ egg mixture into chocolate then add remaining chocolate to egg mixture. Bake in an 8" floured, buttered pyrex dish. Bake at 425° no longer than 15 mins. (center will be liquid). Freeze overnight. Serve with whipped cream and raspberry puree (made from frozen raspberries in sugar sauce). Serves 8.

REFEREE'S NOTE: Suffer gladly!.

NOTES FROM THE BENCH: "It is everything the title suggests. Pure delight to eat. Advised to schedule a 5 mile run immediately after eating and prepare for critical high blood-sugar attack."

Ron Mix

REFEREE'S RELIEF — QUICK CREME DE MENTHE

1 PT. LIME SHERBET

½ PT. VANILLA ICE CREAM

⅓ PT. CREAM, WHIPPED

8 TBSP. CREME DE MENTHE LIQUEUR

Mix sherbet and ice cream until smooth. Blend in whipped cream and creme de menthe. Scoop into champagne glasses and freeze. Serve with a dollop of whipped cream on top and some shaved chocolate. Pass some chocolate cookies around, also.

LEMON BARS

CRUST
1 C. FLOUR
½ C. MARGARINE
¼ C. POWDERED SUGAR

Mix and press in 8x8″ pan, double for 13x9″ pan. Bake 350° for 15 mins.

FILLING
2 BEATEN EGGS
2 TBSP. LEMON JUICE
1 C. SUGAR
2 TBSP. FLOUR
½ TSP. BAKING POWDER

Mix, pour over crust and bake for 25 mins. at 350°. Cool and frost with your favorite cream cheese frosting.

HINT: Lumpy sugar may be softened by placing in a warm oven for 10-15 minutes.

GLAMOROUS STRAWBERRIES JULIET

2½ C. FRESH STRAWBERRIES, CHILLED OR FROZEN
⅓ C. FROZEN WHIPPED DESSERT TOPPING
⅓ C. YOGURT
1 TBSP. SUGAR

Crush ¼ C. of the strawberries; halve the remaining berries. Combine crushed berries, whipped dessert topping (thawed), yogurt, and sugar. Spoon berry halves into 4 sherbet glasses. Top with strawberry-yogurt mixture. Serves 4.

REFEREE'S NOTE: A glamorous finale to your meal — and only 78 calories per serving.

HEATH BAR CAKE

2 C. SIFTED ALL-PURPOSE FLOUR
2 C. BROWN SUGAR, PACKED
1 C. BUTTER OR MARGARINE
1 BEATEN EGG
1 TSP. SODA
1 C. MILK
1 TSP. VANILLA
1 TSP. SALT
½ C. CHOPPED NUTS
6 HEATH CANDY BARS

Grease a 9x13x2″ pan. Chop nuts; crush candy bars. Preheat oven to 350°. Mix flour and sugar, cut in butter until crumbly and reserve 1 C. of this mixture. To remaining amount, add beaten egg, soda, milk, vanilla and salt. Mix thoroughly. Pour into pan. Add nuts to reserved mixture and sprinkle on top of batter. Then sprinkle crushed candy bars over top. Bake for 30-35 mins. Cool on cake rack. Serves 12.

REFEREE'S NOTE: Consumed at a tailgate bash in Cleveland and do those Browns fans know how to eat!

WEDDING LACE CRISPIES

½ C. MARGARINE

1½ C. OLD FASHIONED ROLLED OATS

¾ C. GRANULATED SUGAR

1 TSP. BAKING POWDER

½ TSP. SALT

2 TSP. VANILLA

1 EGG

1 C. PECANS, CUT

Melt margarine and pour over rolled oats. Add sugar, baking powder and salt. Blend with spatula. Add egg, vanilla and nuts. Blend again. Drop by ½ tsp. 2½ inches apart on foil-lined cookie sheet. Bake in 350° oven 10 to 12 mins. until lightly browned. Cool on foil in refrigerator before removing. Makes 6 dozen.

REFEREE'S NOTE: A beautiful end to your buffet spectacular, be it set up in the stadium parking lot or in your home for a reception.

MANDARIN TORTE

1 SM. ANGEL FOOD CAKE

2 - 8 OZ. CANS MANDARIN ORANGES, DRAINED

2 - 3 OZ. PKG. ORANGE GELATIN

2 C. BOILING WATER

1 PT. ORANGE SHERBET

2 C. WHIPPING CREAM, WHIPPED

Tear angel food cake into small pieces. Place in the bottom of 9″ spring form pan. Top with oranges, reserving a few for garnish. Dissolve gelatin in water; add sherbet and stir until dissolved. Chill until slightly thickened; fold in whipped cream. Pour over oranges. Cover with waxed paper. Chill in refrigerator overnight. Remove sides of pan; top the torte with oranges. Serves 8 to 10.

EDITOR'S SPECIAL SHERRY-ALMOND PIE

by Dottie Dekko

1 BAKED 9″ CRUST

¼ C. ALMONDS, CHOPPED AND TOASTED

¼ C. COLD WATER

1 TBSP. UNFLAVORED GELATIN

3 EGG YOLKS

1½ C. MILK

⅓ C. SUGAR

½ TSP. SALT

½ C. WHIPPING CREAM

3 EGG WHITES

¼ C. SUGAR

3 TBSP. SHERRY

½ TSP. ALMOND EXTRACT

1 SQUARE CHOCOLATE

Sprinkle gelatin over water and let stand to soften, about 5 minutes. Beat egg yolks and set aside. Mix milk, sugar and salt in top of double boiler, heat until milk is scalded. Stir in about 3 Tbsp. of hot mixture into egg yolks quickly, then pour into rest of milk mixture and cook until mixture coats a spoon. Remove from heat. Blend in softened gelatin, stirring until gelatin is dissolved. Cool until mixture begins to gel. Whip cream. Beat egg whites until frothy, then add ¼ C. sugar and beat until stiff. Fold whipped cream and egg whites into custard mixture. Fold in Sherry and almonds and turn into pie shell. Chill and serve with chocolate shredded on top.

REFEREE'S NOTE: An elegant pie that I serve only for special friends and family.

SABAYON AUX FRAISES

2 PT. FRESH STRAWBERRIES
SUGAR
1 - 10½ OZ. PKG. FROZEN RASPBERRIES
4 EGG YOLKS
¼ C. GRAND MARNIER
¼ C. SUGAR
½ C. CREAM

PEANUT BUTTER BARS

2 C. PEANUT BUTTER
2½ C. CONFECTIONERS SUGAR
½ C. BROWN SUGAR (PACKED)
½ TSP. VANILLA
1 STICK MARGARINE, SOFT
6 OZ. CHOCOLATE CHIP MORSELS, REAL CHOCOLATE

"REBBETZEN" SOUR CREAM CAKE

¼ LB. BUTTER OR MARGARINE
BREAD CRUMBS, 2 SLICES
1 C. SUGAR
2 EGGS
2 C. FLOUR
1 TSP. BAKING POWDER
1 SCANT TSP. BAKING SODA
1 C. SOUR CREAM
2 TSP. VANILLA
1 TSP. CINNAMON
½ C. BROWN SUGAR
½ C. WALNUTS
½ C. CHOCOLATE CHIPS

Wash and hull strawberries, add sugar to taste and refrigerate until cold. Puree raspberries in blender or processor and put aside. Combine egg yolks, Grand Marnier and sugar in double boiler and beat continuously with a whisk while cooking. Continue until mixture is like whipped cream. Remove pan from hot water and place in iced water. Continue beating until mixture is cold. Whip cream and fold into Sabayon sauce. Refrigerate until ready to serve. Put strawberries into stemmed dessert dish, top with raspberry sauce and a generous spoonful of Sabayon sauce.

REFEREE'S NOTE: Sheer delight from an Oiler's fan.

by PAT LEAHY
(#5, K, New York Jets)

Mix peanut butter, sugars, vanilla and margarine together. Spread in a 9x11" baking pan. Sprinkle on chocolate chips. Bake at 350° for 5 mins. Spread out chocolate on top. Makes 3 dozen bar cookies.

NOTES FROM THE BENCH: "Even peanut butter haters 'love' this one — everyone takes home this recipe."

Pat Leahy

by AUBREY ZELMAN

Cream butter and sugar well. Add eggs. Sift flour, baking powder and baking soda together. Add to butter mixture. Fold in sour cream and vanilla. Fold in chocolate chips. Pour into a 9½" greased spring form pan or bundt pan. Sprinkle with bread crumbs. Mix brown sugar, cinnamon and nuts. Sprinkle over batter. Bake at 350° for 45 mins. to an hour. Voila!

REFEREE'S NOTE: Who is Aubrey Zelman?

DENVER'S MILE HIGH PUDDING PIE

by SUSIE MORTON
(Craig Morton, #7, QB, Denver Broncos)

2 C. FRESH STRAWBERRIES, or 4-5 BANANAS

1 - #2 CAN VANILLA PUDDING OR EQUIVALENT AMOUNT OF COOLED COOKED PUDDING OR SWISS MISS VANILLA PUDDING

1 C. SOUR CREAM

Arrange berries or bananas in cooled cookie crust (recipe to follow). Blend pudding and sour cream together, pour over berries or bananas in crust. Refrigerate 8 hours. Top with whipped cream or glaze (recipe to follow).

GLAZE:

⅓ C. BERRIES OR BANANAS, CRUSHED

⅓ C. SUGAR

1 TBSP. CORNSTARCH

2 TBSP. WATER

Stir together sugar and cornstarch in saucepan. Gradually stir in water and crushed berries or bananas. Boil over medium heat for 1 min., stirring constantly. Cool.

9″ BAKED COOKIE CRUST:

1 C. FLOUR

½ C. (1 STICK) BUTTER OR MARGARINE, SOFTENED

¼ C. PECANS, FINELY CHOPPED

¼ C. CONFECTIONERS SUGAR

Heat oven to 400°. With hands, mix flour, butter or margarine, pecans and sugar until mixture forms a ball. Press firmly and evenly against bottom and side of 9″ pan (not on rim). Bake 10-15 mins. or until very light brown.

"REVERSE PLAY" PEANUT BUTTER PIE

1 ENVELOPE UNFLAVORED GELATIN

¼ C. SUGAR

¼ TSP. SALT

1 C. MILK

2 EGGS, SEPARATED

½ C. PEANUT BUTTER

¼ C. SUGAR

1 C. CREAM, WHIPPED

Combine gelatin, ¼ C. sugar and salt in sauce pan. Add milk and beaten egg yolks; mix well. Cook until boiling and continue to boil for five minutes. Add peanut butter. Place in bowl of ice water or chill until the mixture mounds. Beat egg whites until foamy. Add ¼ C. sugar. Beat until glossy. Fold into peanut butter mixture. Fold in whipped cream. Spoon into pretzel crumb pie shell. (Recipe to follow.) Chill 3 hours.

PRETZEL CRUMB PIE SHELL:

¾ C. PRETZEL CRUMBS

3 TBSP. SUGAR

6 TBSP. MELTED BUTTER

Combine ingredients and press into 9″ pie plate. Bake at 350° for 8 mins.

REFEREE'S NOTE: *A nutty idea with a peanutty taste. An Atlanta nut assured us it's all it's cracked up to be!*

"FIRST ROUND CHOICE" CUPCAKES

3 - 8 OZ. CREAM CHEESE
1 C. SUGAR
5 EGGS
1½ TSP. VANILLA

TOPPING:
1 C. SOUR CREAM
½ C. SUGAR
¼ TSP. VANILLA
DOT OF JELLY

by JANET GRADISHAR
(Randy Gradishar, #53, LB, Denver Broncos)

Mix cream cheese and sugar together. Add beaten eggs, one at a time. Add vanilla. Pour in cupcake holders ¾ full. Bake for 40 mins. in a 300° oven. Cool until depression forms.

Combine first 3 ingredients and top with mixture and add a dot of jelly to the top of each cupcake. Put back in the oven for 5 mins.

REFEREE'S NOTE: These moist, flavorful cupcakes could replace "bread 'n butter" and may become habit-forming!

EDITOR'S WEAKNESS: BANANAS FOSTER

4 BANANAS, QUARTERED LENGTHWISE
1 STICK BUTTER OR MARGARINE
¾ C. BROWN SUGAR
¾ C. FLOUR
½ C. BANANA LIQUEUR
½ C. BRANDY
4 SQUARES OF VANILLA ICE CREAM

by RUTH ARNOLD-KENEFICK

In large saucepan, melt butter and brown sugar over medium heat. Lightly coat quartered bananas in flour and add to butter and sugar mixture. Add banana liqueur and brandy and heat until bananas are heated through. Arrange 4 banana pieces around vanilla ice cream square on plate and top with warm sauce. Serves 4.

REFEREE'S NOTE: A spirited dessert with flair!

"THE DANCELINE'S" PEACH DESSERT

BUTTER BRICKLE CAKE MIX
1 QT. SLICED PEACHES, DRAINED
1 C. CHOPPED PECANS
¾ C. BUTTER

In a 9x13" pan, spread dry cake mix on bottom. Arrange sliced peaches all over on top. Top with chopped pecans. Drizzle butter over all. Bake for 40 mins. in a 350° oven. Top with whipped cream.

REFEREE'S NOTE: Fabulous dessert for a reunion when the "girls get together."

"EXTRA EFFORT" CRANBERRY DESSERT

2 C. FRESH CRANBERRIES, CHOPPED

1 LG. BANANA, 1 C. DICED

½ C. SUGAR

MIX ABOVE 3 ITEMS AND SET ASIDE.

2 C. VANILLA WAFER CRUMBS

6 TBSP. BUTTER, MELTED

½ C. BUTTER

1 C. SUGAR

2 EGGS

½ C. NUTS, CHOPPED

1 C. WHIPPING CREAM

"OUT OF BOUNDS" CHOCOLATE BARS

2 C. FLOUR

1 TSP. BAKING POWDER

1⅓ C. SUGAR

4 TSP. CINNAMON

½ C. BUTTER OR MARGARINE, SOFTENED

¾ C. MILK

1 EGG

1 EGG, SEPARATED

1 C. CHOCOLATE CHIPS

½ C. CHOPPED NUTS

BEST CHOCOLATE MOUSSE IN THE WORLD

¼ C. SUGAR

4 OZ. SEMI-SWEET CHOCOLATE

¼ C. COFFEE CREAM

3 EGG WHITES, STIFFLY BEATEN

2 C. CREAM, WHIPPED

1 TSP. VANILLA

by KEN HOUSTON
(#27, SS, Washington Redskins)

Mix 2 C. wafers and melted butter and press into dish. Cream ½ C. butter and 1 C. sugar until light and fluffy. Fold in ½ C. chopped nuts and spread this mixture over crumb layer. Top this with topping made with cranberries, diced banana and sugar. The last topping is whipped cream. Sprinkle with remaining crumbs. Chill 6 hours.

REFEREE'S NOTE: Tangy, tasty and with lots of zing!

by CHARLIE GETTY
(#77, G-T, Kansas City Chiefs)

Mix and sift flour, baking powder, 1 C. sugar and 3 tsp. cinnamon. Add butter, milk, 1 egg, 1 egg yolk. Blend well on low speed. Spread into lightly greased 9x13″ pan. Beat egg white slightly. Brush over mixture. Combine remaining sugar, cinnamon, chocolate chips, nuts. Sprinkle over top. Bake at 350° for 25 mins.

NOTES FROM THE BENCH: "Good the day after weigh-in!"

Melt chocolate on low heat or in microwave. Add sugar and cream and allow to cool slightly. Add the egg whites, folding in gently. Add whipped cream and then vanilla. Chill thoroughly.

REFEREE'S NOTE: A worthy amount of calories and very simple to prepare.

"ALLEY OOP" HOLIDAY COOKIES

MIX: 1 C. GRANULATED SUGAR

1 C. BROWN SUGAR

⅔ C. COOKING OIL

⅔ C. MARGARINE

3 EGGS

MIX AND ADD: 3½ C. FLOUR

1½ TSP. SALT

1 TSP. VANILLA

ADD: 1 - 12 OZ. PKG. CHOCOLATE CHIPS

OPTIONAL: NUTS, PEANUT BUTTER,
CANDIED FRUIT

by R.C. OWENS

(Former San Francisco Forty Niners WR)

Drop by teaspoons on greased cookie sheet. Bake at 375° for 8 to 10 mins.

REFEREE'S NOTE: This cookie recipe is a great catch for any cookie lover.

R.C. Owens

Q. Which stadium that houses the N.F.L. games has the largest capacity? *Answer page 105.*

"MOM'S" PRETZEL PIE

2 C. CRUSHED PRETZELS

½ C. SUGAR

½ C. BUTTER, MELTED

YOUR FAVORITE ICE CREAM OR SHERBET

Mix all ingredients except ice cream, reserving ½ C. pretzel mixture for topping. Press remaining mixture in 9″ pie tin. Bake at 350° for 12-15 mins. or until brown. Cool. Heap your favorite ice cream or sherbet (different colors gives rainbow effect) in shell and sprinkle on reserved topping. Freeze until ready to serve.

REFEREE'S NOTE: Contributed by an overly enthusiastic Vikings fan who loves to tailgate, but would rather needlepoint than watch the game!

CREAM OF THE CROP — BERRIES 'N CREAM

1 - 15 OZ. CAN CONDENSED MILK

⅓ C. LEMON JUICE (2 OR 3 LEMONS)

1 TBSP. GRATED LEMON RIND

1 PT. STRAWBERRIES

1 C. WHIPPING CREAM

8 LADYFINGERS

In medium bowl, combine first three ingredients. Fold in berries. Whip ½ C. cream until stiff. Fold into mixture. Split ladyfingers and line a loaf pan. Pour berry mixture in pan, keeping fingers in place. Chill at least 3 hours. Remove cake to plate and whip remaining cream. Spread on top and garnish with berries.

REFEREE'S NOTE: An effective, easy dessert. Serve on a large crystal platter with lemon leaves and whole strawberries as a garnish.

MERINGUE AND MACAROON RING

4 EGG WHITES

1 TSP. VANILLA

⅛ TSP. CREAM OF TARTAR

1 C. POWDERED SUGAR, SIFTED

1 C. CRUMBLED MACAROONS

1 PT. HEAVY CREAM

REFEREE'S NOTE: Extra elegant.

Beat egg whites in electric mixer until foamy. Add vanilla and cream of tartar. Add sugar a little at a time, while continuing to beat egg whites. When egg whites are stiff, meringue is ready to bake. Cut brown paper to fit baking sheet. Draw a circle 8¾ inch in diameter and a smaller circle inside 5½ inch diameter. Form meringue on circle and bake as follows: preheat oven to 475°. Put meringue in oven and turn off immediately. Leave in oven 8 hours or overnight. Add crumbled macaroons to cream and let stand for about 1 hour. Beat the mixture until it becomes very thick. Just before serving, place meringue on large platter. Coat the outside generously with macaroon and cream mixture
Fill center with fruit in season.

CARAMEL BROWNIES

1 PACKAGE GERMAN CHOCOLATE CAKE MIX

1 CAN CARNATION MILK

1 - 6 OZ. PKG. CHOCOLATE CHIPS

1 - 4 OZ. PKG. PECAN CHIPS

14 OZ. KRAFT LIGHT CARAMELS

⅔ C. MILK

¾ C. MARGARINE, MELTED

Melt caramels with ⅓ C. milk. Keep warm. Mix cake mix with other ⅓ C. milk and melted margarine, add nuts. Spread ½ mixture in greased 9x13" pan. Bake at 350° for 6 mins. Take from oven, pour caramel mixture over. Sprinkle with chocolate chips. Cover with remaining dough, dropped by teaspoon. Return to oven and spread this dough out as it softens from the heat. Close oven door and continue to bake 17 to 20 mins. more. Do not over bake. Refrigerate 30 mins. before serving.

REFEREE'S NOTE: A favorite of fans everywhere.

CELEBRATION STRAWBERRIES ROMANOFF

3 C. SOUR CREAM

1 C. BROWN SUGAR

⅓ C. COINTREAU

WHOLE STRAWBERRIES

Wash and stem fresh strawberries and put in champagne glasses. Beat remaining ingredients together and pour over berries.

REFEREE'S NOTE: Guaranteed to create a feeling of well-being and celebration.

"SWEET VICTORY" CARAMELS

2 C. SUGAR

1¾ C. LIGHT CORN SYRUP

2 C. WHIPPING CREAM

¼ LB. BUTTER

DASH SALT

1 TSP. VANILLA

by BILL KOLLAR

(#77, DE-DT, Tampa Bay Buccaneers)

Cook sugar, light corn syrup, 1 C. cream and butter slowly to boil. Then add remaining cream slowly. Boil till reaches soft ball stage. Add salt and vanilla (and nuts if desired). Pour into greased jelly roll pan. Do not scrape last of syrup from pan.

REFEREE'S NOTE: What a sweet taste of victory!

Bill Kollar

HINT: Briefly warm shelled nuts before chopping — it brings out the natural nut oils.

YUMMY TOFFEE

2 C. BUTTER

2 C. SUGAR

2 C. SALTED ALMONDS, COARSELY CHOPPED

6 TBSP. WATER

2 TBSP. LIGHT CORN SYRUP

1 TSP. VANILLA

8 OZ. MILK CHOCOLATE

REFEREE'S NOTE: These yummy morsels catch the spirit of the holiday season — pile them up on a plate, wrap a bow around it all and give it as divine gift.

Start melting butter in a heavy 2 qt. saucepan over low heat. Gradually add sugar, stirring constantly. Blend in 1 C. almonds, water and corn syrup. Set candy thermometer in place. Cook over medium heat, stirring a few times, until temperature reaches 300°. Remove from heat and stir in vanilla. Quickly pour into buttered 15½x10½x1″ pan and spread to corners. When candy has cooled slightly, mark into squares with a sharp knife. Cool. Meanwhile, melt chocolate over hot water. Cool. When candy is completely cool, spread melted chocolate evenly over top. Sprinkle remaining nuts over chocolate. When chocolate is set, break toffee into pieces. Store in a tightly covered container. Makes about 3 lbs. of toffee.

THE SIDE LINERS

"MOVING POCKET" TURKEY STUFFING

2 BAGS SEASONED BREAD CRUMBS

4 C. CELERY, DICED

2 ONIONS, DICED

2 CANS CONSOMME

2 C. MUSHROOMS, DICED

SALT AND PEPPER

1 LB. SAUSAGE, FRIED AND REMOVED FROM CASING

HUSH PUPPIES

3 C. CORN MEAL

¼ C. FLOUR

4 TSP. BAKING POWDER

1 TSP. SALT

1 TSP. RED PEPPER

2 HOT PEPPERS, FINELY CUT

1½ C. BUTTERMILK

1 C. AMERICAN CHEESE, GRATED

4 EGGS

"FLYING WEDGE" BANANA BREAD

3½ C. FLOUR

2½ TSP. BAKING POWDER

1 TSP. BAKING SODA

1½ TSP. SALT

⅔ C. SHORTENING

1⅓ C. SUGAR

4 EGGS, SLIGHTLY BEATEN

2 C. BANANAS, MASHED — 4 to 6 BANANAS

by RAY MALAVASI

(Head Coach, Los Angeles Rams)

Blend all the ingredients and stuff the turkey.

REFEREE'S NOTE: Coach Malavasi knows what should go on the "sidelines" and this winner will make your dinner into a championship occasion.

Ray Malavasi

by HOWARD SAMPSON

(#36, S, Green Bay Packers)

Combine all the ingredients, mix well. Then use cooking oil and heat it in a deep fryer at about 450°. Dip hush-puppy mix out of bowl with a tablespoon for desired size. Drop in deep fryer, cook until ready to eat. Drain on a paper towel.

NOTES FROM THE BENCH: "Because I do like to cook, this was an enjoyable recipe for me to contribute and I hope you enjoy it as much as I did!"

REFEREE'S NOTE: If you are a cheese lover, add more.

by MARK KONCAR

(#79, T, Green Bay Packers)

Sift flour, measure, add baking powder, soda and salt. Sift again. Cream shortening, add sugar gradually. Continue beating until light and fluffy. Add eggs and mix until smooth. Add dry ingredients alternately with the mashed bananas, stirring just enough to combine thoroughly. Do not beat. Turn into 2 - 9½x5½" greased loaf pans or several small pans and bake in moderate oven 350° for about an hour.

NOTES FROM THE BENCH: "Especially good served warm with fresh butter."

Mark Koncar

"ON TARGET" SQUASH

3 C. ZUCCHINI SQUASH, SLICED

2 TBSP. ONION, CHOPPED

2 LG. TOMATOES, SKINNED AND SLICED

2 TBSP. BUTTER

1 TSP. SALT

¼ TSP. OREGANO, OPTIONAL

½ LB. MOZZARELLA CHEESE, SHREDDED

GREEN BEANS CAN BE SUBSTITUTED
FOR SQUASH

by MAXINE FINKS
(Jim Finks, General Manager, Chicago Bears)

Simmer gently in water to cover zucchini and onion until barely tender, about 4 mins. Drain thoroughly. Arrange in baking dish. Arrange sliced, skinned tomatoes on top, drizzle with butter. Sprinkle with salt and oregano. Top with cheese. Bake in a moderate oven, 350°, for 30 mins.

REFEREE'S NOTE: A colorful array of nutrition.

Maxine Finks

COACH GIBRON'S CORN PUDDING

1 CAN CREAMED CORN

2 HEAPING TBSP. BROWN SUGAR

1 TBSP. FLOUR

3 TBSP. BUTTER, MELTED

3 EGGS

SALT AND PEPPER

by ABE GIBRON
(Assistant Head Coach, Tampa Bay Buccaneers)

Mix together all ingredients and pour into greased casserole. Bake at 350° for 45 mins.

REFEREE'S NOTE: Great on the sidelines for any dinner.

Abe Gibron

"FLANKER" STEAK MARINADE

3 TBSP. SCALLIONS OR SHALLOTS, MINCED

1½ TBSP. SOY SAUCE

2 TBSP. OLIVE OIL

JUICE OF ½ LEMON

LARGE PINCH PEPPER OR 2 DROPS TABASCO SAUCE

½ TSP. THYME OR ITALIAN SEASONING

Spread on both sides of meat in flat pan. Keep turning, but keep covered with waxed paper.

OTTO'S GREEN BEANS SUPREME

2 - 10 OZ. PKGS. GREEN BEANS, FRENCH STYLE

2 TBSP. FLOUR

2 TBSP. BUTTER OR MARGARINE

1 C. SOUR CREAM

1 C. SWISS CHEESE, GRATED

BREAD CRUMBS

by OTTO GRAHAM
(Hall of Fame, Former Cleveland Browns QB)

While green beans are boiling in salted water, make white sauce in top of double boiler. Melt cheese in white sauce. Combine with green beans in a good-sized casserole. Cover with bread crumbs in melted butter.

REFEREE'S NOTE: *"Automatic Otto" not only knows his plays but his green beans!*

Otto Graham

"SPLIT THE UPRIGHTS" CHEESE BREAD

1 LOAF UNSLICED BAKERY BREAD

1 STICK MARGARINE OR BUTTER, MELTED

1 TBSP. MUSTARD

1 TSP. POPPY SEEDS

SWISS CHEESE, SLICED

4 SLICES BACON

by EMERSON BOOZER
(Former New York Jets HB)

Cut top and side crusts off bread and cut into slices but do not cut through bottom crust. Mix margarine, mustard and poppy seeds and brush between slices of bread and top. Place piece of cheese between each slice and press loaf into shape and place four slices of bacon on top. Bake 20 mins. at 350°.

REFEREE'S NOTE: *Inventive and hearty!*

JOHN BRODIE'S MUSHROOMS AU GRATIN

1 LB. FRESH MUSHROOMS

2 TBSP. BUTTER

⅓ C. SOUR CREAM

¼ TSP. SALT

DASH PEPPER

1 TBSP. FLOUR

¼ C. PARSLEY

½ C. SWISS OR MILD CHEDDAR CHEESE, SHREDDED

NOTES FROM THE BENCH: *"This has become a family dish used for special holidays such as Thanksgiving. I usually double or triple it."*

by SUE BRODIE
(John Brodie, Sportscaster NBC, Former San Francisco Forty Niners QB)

Wash and slice mushrooms lengthwise through the stem into about ¼" thick slices. Heat butter in frying pan, then saute mushrooms until lightly browned. Cover pan for about 2 mins. until they exude juice. Blend the sour cream with salt, pepper, and flour until smooth. Stir into the mushrooms in the pan and heat, stirring until blended and beginning to boil. Pour into a shallow, rimmed oven-proof plate. Sprinkle parsley and cheese evenly on top. You can do this much in advance and refrigerate until dinner time. Shortly before serving, place uncovered in a 425° oven until mushrooms are heated and cheese melted, approximately 10 mins. Serves 4.

Sue Brodie

"SQUASHED" CASSEROLE

2 C. SQUASH, COOKED AND DRAINED
½ C. MAYONNAISE
½ C. ONION, CHOPPED
1 EGG
1 TSP. SUGAR
1 C. CHEESE, GRATED
½ STICK MARGARINE
SALT AND PEPPER TO TASTE
20 CRACKERS, CRUMBLED

by PAGE HANNAH
(John Hannah, #73, G, New England Patriots)

Cook, drain and mash squash. Mix mayonnaise, onion and egg together and add to squash. Add salt, pepper and sugar. Brown cracker crumbs in margarine. Put squash in baking dish sprayed with oil, and sprinkle with cheese, then browned cracker crumbs. Cook at 350° for about 30 mins.

Q. The name "Scramblin' Man" refers to what former player who now wields the microphone rather than the pigskin? *Answer page 105.*

BROCCOLI A LA CONN

2 PKG. FROZEN CHOPPED BROCCOLI
1 STICK MARGARINE OR BUTTER
½ LB. VELVEETA CHEESE, GRATED
¼ LB. RITZ CRACKERS

by SHARON CONN
(Dick Conn, #22, S, New England Patriots)

Cook broccoli according to package directions. Combine ½ stick of butter and cheese with broccoli. Pour into buttered casserole dish. Crush crackers and add ½ stick of melted butter. Mix thoroughly. Sprinkle over top of casserole. Bake 20-30 mins. at 350°.

REFEREE'S NOTE: *This is a sure bet, and a safe play.*

HINT: Use your blender to make cookie and bread crumbs in a hurry.

"STACK 'EM UP" CORN BREAD MUFFINS

1-1½ C. SELF-RISING CORNMEAL
¾ C. FLOUR
1 TSP. SUGAR
1½ C. COLD SWEET MILK
4 TBSP. MARGARINE, MELTED

by BOB JOHNSON
(Former Cincinnati Bengals C)

Add ingredients in order given, mix well. Pour mixture into well-greased and preheated muffin tin cups, filling each about half-full. Bake at 450° for 30 mins.

REFEREE'S NOTE: *For a "one on one" compliment, stack these up with butter and a glass of cold milk.*

POTATO AND SOUR CREAM BLITZ

½ C. SOUR CREAM

6 GREEN ONIONS

8-10 POTATOES, PEELED

8 OZ. CREAM CHEESE, SOFTENED

½ STICK BUTTER, MELTED

by JAN STENERUD
(#3, K, Kansas City Chiefs)

Cook potatoes in boiling, salted water until tender. Drain. Beat cream cheese, sour cream and onions with a mixer until well blended. Stir in hot potatoes and butter until fluffy. Salt and pepper to taste. Transfer to a 2 qt. buttered baking dish and bake at 350° for 30 mins.

REFEREE'S NOTE: *Blitz your company with this impressive side dish.*

NOTES FROM THE BENCH: *"Absolutely the best potatoes in the world!"*

Jan Stenerud

SOUR CREAM AND ZUCCHINI

ZUCCHINI

SOUR CREAM

CHEDDAR CHEESE, GRATED

PARMESAN CHEESE, GRATED

Cut zucchini into 4" hunks and boil until tender. Slice in half lengthwise. Scoop out seeds and spread with sour cream. Sprinkle with two cheeses. Bake at 350° until cheese melts.

"SUPERSTAR" SOUR CREAM COFFEE CAKE

by JULIE HAYNES
(Mike Haynes, #40, CB-KR, New England Patriots)

Cream butter and sugar well. Add eggs, one at a time, beating well. Sift dry ingredients, add alternately with sour cream and blend well. Add vanilla. To make topping mix brown sugar, flour and cinnamon in another bowl and cut in butter with pastry blender or 2 knives. Add nuts. Pour ½ batter into greased mold, sprinkle with ½ topping. Add other half of batter and top with remaining topping. Bake in 300 ° oven for 50 mins. in 9 C. mold, and 60 mins. in the 12 C. mold.

REFEREE'S NOTE: *The superstar of coffee-cakes.*

BATTER	9 CUP	12 CUP
BUTTER OR MARGARINE	½ C.	¾ C.
SUGAR	1 C.	1½ C.
EGGS	3	5
SIFTED FLOUR	2 C.	3 C.
BAKING SODA	1 TSP.	1½ TSP.
BAKING POWDER	1 TSP.	1½ TSP.
DAIRY SOUR CREAM	8 OZ.	8 OZ.
VANILLA	1 TSP.	1½ TSP.
TOPPING:		
BROWN SUGAR	¾ C.	1 C.
FLOUR	2 TBSP.	3 TBSP.
CINNAMON	¾ TSP.	1 TSP.
BUTTER OR MARGARINE	2 TBSP.	3 TBSP.
CHOPPED NUTS	½ C.	¾ C.

"FIRST CHOICE" GULLIVERS CREAMED CORN

2 PKGS. FROZEN WHOLE KERNEL CORN, THAWED

3 C. CREAM

½ C. SUGAR

1 TBSP. SALT

1 TSP. M.S.G.

½ C. BUTTER

½ C. FLOUR

by VIVIAN NICCOLAI

(Armand Niccolai, Former Pittsburgh Pirates K)

Cook corn using all the cream instead of water. After the corn is cooked, strain corn and set aside. Fold remaining ingredients into cream. Cream should still be warm to melt the butter. Stir. Pour creamy mixture into corn.

NOTES FROM THE BENCH: *"The corn has a very delicate flavor and is popular at dinner at our home."*

Vivian A. Niccolai

SPICED MOCHA COFFEE

½ C. WHIPPING CREAM

1 TSP. INSTANT COFFEE POWDER

1 TBSP. SUGAR

¼ TSP. GROUND CINNAMON

6 TBSP. CHOCOLATE SYRUP

FRESHLY MADE HOT COFFEE

NUTMEG

In small mixer bowl, combine whipping cream, instant coffee, sugar, cinnamon and dash of nutmeg. Whip until stiff peaks form. Put 1 Tbsp. chocolate syrup in each of 6 coffee cups. Fill cups with hot coffee. Stir gently to mix. Top with generous spoonfuls of the whipped cream mixture.

REFEREE'S NOTE: *A Detroit fan witnessed this being served at a bitterly cold tailgate and watched the party warm up!*

HERB SPINACH BAKE

1 - 10 OZ. PKG. FROZEN CHOPPED SPINACH

1 C. COOKED RICE

1 C. SHARP CHEDDAR CHEESE, SHREDDED

2 EGGS, SLIGHTLY BEATEN

2 TBSP. MELTED BUTTER OR MARGARINE

⅓ C. MILK

2 TBSP. ONION, CHOPPED

½ TSP. WORCESTERSHIRE SAUCE

1 TSP. SALT

¼ TSP. ROSEMARY, CRUSHED OR THYME LEAVES, CRUSHED

Cook and drain spinach. Mix with 1 C. cooked rice. Combine ingredients. Pour mixture into 10x6x1½" baking dish. Bake in moderate oven, 350°, 20 to 25 mins. or until knife inserted halfway between center and edge comes out clean. Cut in squares. Serves 6.

REFEREE'S NOTE: *A delicate flavor for spinach fanciers and those who aren't sure if they even "like" spinach. Try it, you'll love it!*

"SIDELINERS" SHERRIED MUSHROOMS FOR STEAK

½ LB. FRESH MUSHROOMS

1 GREEN ONION, CHOPPED

5 TBSP. BUTTER

SALT AND PEPPER TO TASTE

¼ C. DRY SHERRY

PINCH TARRAGON

Rinse mushrooms lightly; drain well and trim stems. Cut into thick slices. Heat 4 Tbsp. butter until foam has subsided. Add mushrooms and chopped onion. Saute just until tender. Remove to bowl with slotted spoon. Salt and pepper. To skillet drippings, add Sherry and reduce heat to low; add pinch of tarragon and remaining 1 Tbsp. butter. Cook 1 min. Add mushrooms and heat carefully. Taste for seasoning, then pour over hot steaks. Serves 2.

"INTERCEPTED" BAKED POTATOES

3-4 LG. BAKING POTATOES

¾ C. SOUR CREAM

1 TBSP. ONION, GRATED

1½ TSP. SALT

3 TBSP. BUTTER

½ C. CHEDDAR CHEESE, SHREDDED

by HAROLD CARMICHAEL

(#17, WR, Philadelphia Eagles)

Bake potatoes until tender, about 1 hour in a 400° oven. Cut potatoes in half lengthwise. Scoop out potato and set shells aside or use foil potato holders. In mixing bowl, whip potatoes; add sour cream, onion, salt and butter. Beat until fluffy. Fold in cheese. Divide into shells. Return to oven 12-15 mins. or until hot and lightly browned. Serve immediately. Serves 6-8.

REFEREE'S NOTE: Intercept your ordinary baked potatoes to really turn your dinner around.

Harold Carmichael

"QUICK SCREEN" BLACK BEANS

5 TBSP. OIL

1½ GREEN PEPPER

1 LG. ONION

2 GARLIC CLOVES

1 TSP. PAPRIKA

1 BAY LEAF

1 - 6 OZ. CAN TOMATO SAUCE

2 CANS BLACK BEANS

OREGANO

by MARIA NELSON

(Steve Nelson, #57, LB, New England Patriots)

Heat oil in skillet. Finely chop pepper, onion and garlic. Add dash of oregano, bay leaf, paprika and saute over medium heat until golden brown. Add the 2 cans of black beans and ½ can water. Cook over medium until boiling, stirring constantly. Serve over rice.

REFEREE'S NOTE: Earthy and robust!

WASSAIL PUNCH BOWL

1 GAL. APPLE CIDER

1 QT. CRANBERRY JUICE

1 SM. CAN FROZEN ORANGE JUICE CONCENTRATE

1 SM. CAN LEMONADE MIX CONCENTRATE

3 WHOLE ORANGES, STUDDED WITH CLOVES

6 STICKS CINNAMON

2 TSP. AROMATIC BITTERS*

1 TBSP. WHOLE CLOVES*

1 TBSP. WHOLE ALLSPICE

2 C. RUM OR SOUTHERN COMFORT OR TO TASTE

*In cloth bag.

In saucepan, combine cider, cranberry juice, orange juice, lemonade mix, whole oranges, bitters and spices. Simmer 10 mins. or longer. Remove spice bag, oranges and cinnamon sticks. Stir in rum or Southern Comfort and pour into punch bowl. Float oranges on top. Serves 25.

REFEREE'S NOTE: No penalty for spending too much time in the huddle around the punch bowl!

HINT: Heat lemons or limes in hot water for a few minutes before squeezing and you'll get much more juice.

MORNING SMILE

6 OZ. ICE COLD ORANGE JUICE

1 OZ. VODKA

1 OZ. HONEY

1 EGG

Blend all ingredients.

REFEREE'S NOTE: This drink lends nutrition as well as smiles to morning gatherings.

HINT: Add a few pieces of chocolate to coffee for a delicious mocha flavor — or try sprinkling cinnamon on the grounds before perking for a subtle added flavor.

"PRE-SEASON" PEAS IN SOUR CREAM

1 - 10 OZ. PKG. FROZEN GREEN PEAS

1 LG. CUCUMBER, SEEDED, PARED AND SLICED THIN

2 TBSP. WATER

1 TSP. TARRAGON LEAVES

1 TSP. SALT

½ C. SOUR CREAM

2 TBSP. LEMON JUICE

½ C. MAYONNAISE

Combine peas, cucumber, water, tarragon and salt in heavy saucepan; cover tightly and cook 5-7 mins. Drain. Combine sour cream, lemon juice and mayonnaise in another pan. Warm over very low heat, stirring constantly. Stir peas and cucumber into sauce. Serve immediately. Serves 4 to 6.

GOURMET WILD RICE

2 C. UNCOOKED WILD RICE

4 C. WATER

2 TSP. SALT

2 LB. LEAN GROUND BEEF

1 LB. FRESH MUSHROOMS

½ C. CHOPPED CELERY

1 C. CHOPPED ONION

½ C. BUTTER

¼ C. SOY SAUCE

2 C. DAIRY SOUR CREAM

2 TSP. SALT, OR LESS

¼ TSP. PEPPER

½ C. SLIVERED ALMONDS (SAVE SOME FOR GARNISH)

Gently cook wild rice in water and 2 tsp. salt, (covered) for 45 mins. Drain if necessary. Brown ground beef. Rinse mushrooms, cut off tips of stems, slice caps and saute with onions and celery in butter for 5 mins. Combine soy sauce, sour cream, salt and pepper. Add cooked wild rice, beef, onion, mushrooms and celery mixture and almonds. Toss lightly. Place mixture in lightly greased 3 qt. casserole. Bake in a moderate oven, 350°, for about an hour, uncovered. Add water if needed and season to taste. Stir several times. Garnish with reserved almonds. Serves 12-16.

REFEREE'S NOTE: *Ah — wild rice — treasured by connoisseurs, and it should be, for it costs the earth and is about as available as a Super Bowl ticket!*

"PLAY OFF" PUNCH

¼ C. SUGAR

½ TSP. CINNAMON

¼ TSP. GINGER

6 EGGS

1 QT. CHILLED ORANGE JUICE

1 QT. CHILLED PINEAPPLE JUICE

1 QT. CHILLED GINGER ALE

ORANGE SHERBET, OPTIONAL

by PAT MINER

(Tom Miner, Scout, Cleveland Browns)

Mix sugar and spices. Add eggs; beat well. Stir in chilled juices and ginger ale, blending thoroughly. Add scoops of sherbet, if desired. Makes approximately 24-½ cup servings. Note: without the orange sherbet, it makes a great breakfast drink.

CHAMPAGNE CHIC

SOUTHERN COMFORT, CHILLED

CHAMPAGNE, CHILLED

TWIST LEMON

In chilled champagne glasses, fill stem with chilled Southern Comfort. If glasses do not have hollow stems, put in ¼ oz. (thimble full) of Southern Comfort. Fill to brim with chilled champagne. Add twist of lemon.

REFEREE'S NOTE: *From a loyal fan whose culinary credentials are superb.*

"STIFF ARM" CHAMPAGNE PUNCH

2 LEMONS, SLICED VERY THIN

2 ORANGES, SLICED VERY THIN

1 BOX FROZEN PINEAPPLE

1½ C. SUGAR

1 C. APPLEJACK

½ C. TRIPLE SEC

1 JAR MARASCHINO CHERRIES WITH JUICE

6 BOTTLES CHILLED CALIFORNIA CHAMPAGNE

Slice fruit with rinds on. Combine fruit with other ingredients, except champagne, and let stand overnight. When you are ready to serve the punch, put a large block of ice in your punch bowl and pour the mixture over it. Add the champagne.

PINEAPPLE CARROT BREAD

MIX IN ORDER:

3 EGGS, BEATEN

2 C. SUGAR

1¼ C. OIL

2 C. CARROTS, GRATED

1 - 20 OZ. CAN CRUSHED PINEAPPLE, DRAINED

1 TSP. SALT

1½ TSP. CINNAMON

1 TSP. SODA

3 C. FLOUR

Fill 2 loaf pans which have been lined with wax paper or plain brown paper. (Do not grease.) Bake at 350° for about 1 hour and 10 mins.

REFEREE'S NOTE: Contributed by a fussy fan.

EGGNOG WASSAIL PRO BOWL

3 QTS. DAIRY EGGNOG

½ TSP. NUTMEG

4 WHOLE CLOVES

½ TSP. CINNAMON

1½ QTS. APPLE CIDER

WHIPPED CREAM

1 TSP. GRATED LEMON PEEL

NUTMEG

Combine eggnog, cider, nutmeg, cinnamon, cloves and lemon peel in saucepan. Heat over low heat, stirring occasionally. Serve hot or chilled with a dollop of whipped cream and sprinkle of nutmeg.

REFEREE'S NOTE: A rich, golden treat.

MUSHROOM BUSINESS

1 LB. FRESH MUSHROOMS, SLICED

8 SLICES BREAD, CUBED

½ C. ONION, CHOPPED

½ C. CELERY, SLICED

½ C. GREEN PEPPER, CHOPPED

½ C. MAYONNAISE

¾ TSP. SALT

¼ TSP. PEPPER

2 EGGS, SLIGHTLY BEATEN

1½ C. MILK

1 CAN MUSHROOM SOUP

CHEDDAR CHEESE, GRATED

Saute mushrooms in butter just until they start to smell like mushrooms. Put 3 slices of bread, cubed, into casserole. Combine mushrooms with onion, celery, green pepper, mayonnaise, salt and pepper and spread on bread cubes. Add 3 slices bread, cubed, on top. Add eggs to milk and pour over. Refrigerate at least 1 hour. One hour before serving, spoon 1 can undiluted mushroom soup over casserole and 2 more slices of bread, cubed. Bake at 350° for 50-60 mins. Sprinkle cheese on top just before serving. 6-8 servings.

REFEREE'S NOTE: *Add a little fun and flavor to business.*

ORIENTAL RICE

3 TBSP. BUTTER

3 C. COOKED RICE

⅛ TSP. CURRY POWDER

⅓ C. PARSLEY, CHOPPED

1 TSP. SALT

¼ C. TOASTED ALMONDS

Melt butter, add curry and blend. Combine with rice. Add parsley, salt and toasted almonds. Place in casserole. Heat in moderate oven at 350° for 20-25 mins.

REFEREE'S NOTE: *Revamp the rice routine with an oriental accent.*

"WEDGE BUSTER" ONION-PARMESAN BREAD

½ C. GRATED PARMESAN CHEESE

½ C. MAYONNAISE OR SALAD DRESSING

¼ C. ONION, FINELY CHOPPED

LOAF OF FRENCH BREAD

Combine Parmesan cheese, mayonnaise and onion. Slice French bread in half lengthwise. Spread cut surfaces of bread with Parmesan-onion mixture. Place on baking sheet; bake in moderate oven, 375°, for 15 to 18 mins. or till bubbly and brown. Cut in pieces. Serves 10.

REFEREE'S NOTE: *Try it in your "outdoor oven" — wrap in foil and toss it on the grill.*

81

CHEESED BROCCOLI

2 PKG. FROZEN CHOPPED BROCCOLI, COOKED AND DRAINED

1 CAN CREAM OF MUSHROOM SOUP

½ C. MAYONNAISE

1 TBSP. LEMON JUICE

½ C. SHARP CHEESE, GRATED

1 JAR CHOPPED PIMENTO

1 C. CRUSHED CHEESE CRACKERS

¼ C. SLIVERED ALMONDS OR PECANS

Place broccoli in 2 qt. casserole. Mix soup, mayonnaise, lemon juice and cheese; spoon over top of broccoli. Top with pimento, crackers and nuts. Bake in 350° oven 20 mins. Serves 8-10.

HINT: Cauliflower will not turn yellow if you add ½ cup of milk to the cooking water.

HOT CURRIED FRUIT

1 - 1 LB. 3 OZ. CAN PEACH SLICES

1 - 1 LB. 10 OZ. CAN PEAR HALVES

1 - 1 LB. CAN PINEAPPLE CHUNKS

1 - 1 LB. CAN PITTED BING CHERRIES

1 - 1 LB. 13 OZ. CAN APRICOTS

1 C. BROWN SUGAR, PACKED

1 TSP. CURRY POWDER

¼ LB. MARGARINE

Drain fruit well and mix. Put into a 9x13″ pan. Melt brown sugar, curry powder and margarine; pour over mixed fruit. Heat in a 300° oven for 30 mins., being sure the fruit neither burns nor cooks too long. It is only necessary to heat the fruit through. Serve hot or margarine will solidify. To stretch recipe, use 2 cans peaches and 2 cans of pears and another recipe of sugar mixture. Serves 15.

GINGER BANANA BREAD

⅔ C. SUGAR

⅓ C. SHORTENING

2 EGGS

1⅓ C. FLOUR

2¾ TSP. BAKING POWDER

½ TSP. SALT

⅞ C. BANANAS, MASHED

¼ C. GINGER MARMALADE

Blend sugar and shortening. Add eggs and beat until fluffy. Combine flour, baking powder and salt. Mash bananas and add marmalade. Add dry ingredients to sugar mixture alternately with banana mixture and blend well. Pour into a greased and paper lined loaf pan. Bake at 350° for 70 mins. Cool bread in pan for 20 mins. and then slice and serve warm with butter.

REFEREE'S NOTE: Appeared at a tailgate in Oakland and the hamper was raided.

IRRESISTIBLE COFFEE CAKE

DRY INGREDIENTS

1 C. BROWN SUGAR

1 C. WHITE SUGAR

1 C. BUTTER

1 TSP. CINNAMON

2 C. FLOUR

MIX THE ABOVE INGREDIENTS AND RESERVE.

2 EGGS

1 C. BUTTERMILK

1 TSP. SODA

1 C. NUTS, CHOPPED

Beat ingredients, except nuts, and add to ½ of the dry ingredients. Sprinkle nuts on bottom of greased 9x12″ pan. Pour ½ batter in pan and add ½ C. reserved dry mix. Add rest of batter, then rest of dry ingredients. Refrigerate over night. Bake at 350° for 40-45 mins.

REFEREE'S NOTE: *Contributed by a Bronco's fan who could not resist.*

Q. Which Super Bowl set the attendance record?
Answer page 105.

KENNY'S PINTO BEANS

2 C. DRIED PINTO BEANS

6 C. WATER

1 TBSP. SALT

1 TBSP. PEPPER

1 TBSP. GARLIC POWDER

1 MED. GREEN BELL PEPPER, CHOPPED

1 MED. ONION, CHOPPED

2 RIBS OF CELERY, CHOPPED

1 LB. GROUND BEEF

2 TBSP. CHILI POWDER

by KEN HOUSTON
(#27, SS, Washington Redskins)

Soak beans overnight in 6 C. of water. Next morning, drain beans and place in large pot and add 6 C. fresh water. Add salt, pepper, garlic powder and ½ of onion, garlic, bell pepper, and celery mixture. Bring to a boil and then turn fire down and cook slowly for 2 hours or until beans are tender. Add more boiling water if needed. Always keep about 3 inches of water above the beans during the first hour. In a large skillet, brown lean ground beef (no oil) onion, celery, green pepper and garlic mixture. Pour off grease, if any, and add to the bean mixture plus 2 Tbsp. of chili powder. Let simmer ½ hour and season to taste. Salt pork, ham or bacon may be added during cooking for extra flavor. Makes 6 cups.

NOTES FROM THE BENCH: *"Very tasty on cold nights — a good meal for the winter season."*

Kenneth R. Houston

(broken right arm)

BROCCOLI RICE CASSEROLE

2 LB. BROCCOLI, COOKED AND DRAINED

¾ C. MINUTE RICE, COOKED

½ C. ONION, CHOPPED

½ C. CELERY, CHOPPED

2 TBSP. BUTTER

1 CAN CREAM OF MUSHROOM SOUP

1 SMALL JAR CHEESE WHIZ

by PAT LEAHY

(#5, K, New York Jets)

Cook onion and celery in butter until soft. Add to rice and soup. Put into casserole. Layer broccoli and cheese on top. Bake at 350° for 45 mins. Cover 30 mins., uncover last 15.

REFEREE'S NOTES: A "winning" combo that's sure to bring compliments.

Pat Leahy

GREEN AND GOLD CASSEROLE

2 - 10 OZ. PKGS. FROZEN CHOPPED SPINACH, COOKED AND DRAINED

1 - 5 OZ. CAN WATER CHESTNUTS, DRAINED AND THINLY SLICED (⅔ C.)

1 - 10 OZ. PKG. FROZEN WELSH RAREBIT, THAWED

8 SLICES BACON, CRISP-COOKED, DRAINED AND CRUMBLED

½ of 3½ OZ. CAN FRENCH FRIED ONION RINGS

Combine spinach, water chestnuts, and one-third of the Welsh rarebit in a 10x6x1½" baking dish. Top with crumbled bacon. Spread remaining rarebit evenly over all; top with onion rings. Bake, uncovered, in moderate oven, 350° for 15 mins. or until heated through. Serves 6.

REFEREE'S NOTE: Tasted at a tailgate in Green Bay, of course.

"FIRST STRING" GREEN BEANS

1½ LB. GREEN BEANS

6 TBSP. BUTTER

2 CLOVES GARLIC

1 TSP. NUTMEG

3 TBSP. PARMESAN CHEESE, GRATED

ALMONDS

Cook green beans. Heat butter and add garlic and nutmeg. Cook 1 min. longer. Place hot vegetable in bowl and pour sauce over. Sprinkle on cheese or almonds.

REFEREE'S NOTE: Add this to your array of colorful condiments that compliment your tailgate cookery.

BO BOLINGER'S RED HOT CORN BREAD

1 - 8 OZ. CAN CREAMED CORN

¾ C. MILK

⅓ C. VEGETABLE SHORTENING, MELTED

1½ C. YELLOW CORN MEAL

2 EGGS, SLIGHTLY BEATEN

1 TSP. BAKING POWDER

1 TSP. SALT

1 TSP. SUGAR

½ TSP. BAKING SODA

1½ C. LONGHORN CHEDDAR CHEESE, GRATED

TO BLOCK THAT KICK: 1 - 4 OZ. CAN CHOPPED GREEN CHILIES

FOR AN ON-SIDE KICK: 1 - 6 OZ. CAN JALPENO PEPPERS, CHOPPED

by BO BOLINGER
(Scout, St. Louis Cardinals)

In a large mixing bowl, combine all ingredients except cheese and chilies. Mix well. Gradually add chilies or peppers and grated cheese, blending until smooth. Pour into lightly greased 8x11" baking pan. Bake at 375° for 30 mins.

Bo Bolinger

HINT: To cut fresh bread more easily, warm the knife.

"END ZONE" ZUCCHINI CAKE

3 EGGS

1 C. OIL

2 C. SUGAR

2 C. RAW ZUCCHINI, UNPEELED AND GRATED

1 TSP. VANILLA

3 C. FLOUR

1 TSP. SALT

½ TSP. BAKING POWDER

3 TSP. CINNAMON

1 TSP. BAKING SODA

½ C. NUTS, CHOPPED

by VIVIAN NICCOLAI
(Armand Niccolai, Former Pittsburgh Pirates K)

Beat eggs well until light. Add oil, sugar, zucchini and vanilla. Mix well. Add dry ingredients and mix well until blended. Pour into well greased and floured loaf pans (2). Bake 1 hour at 350°. Slice and serve with whipped cream. Serves 12 generous slices.

"TEAM UP" CORN AND TOMATOES

1 - 3 OZ. CAN FRENCH FRIED ONION RINGS

1 TOMATO, SLICED THIN

½ TSP. SUGAR

¼ TSP. SALT

1 CAN CORN

¼ TSP. CELERY SEED

Butter casserole. Spread ½ can onion rings on bottom. Arrange tomato slices on top. Sprinkle with sugar and salt. Spoon on corn. Sprinkle with celery seed, add remaining onion rings, dot with butter and bake at 350° for 15 mins.

HINT: Fresh tomatoes keep longer when stored with stem ends down.

FAN PLEASING POTATO CASSEROLE

2 BOXES FROZEN HASH BROWN POTATOES

1 JAR PARMESAN CHEESE, SHREDDED

1 PT. WHIPPING CREAM

Place potatoes in greased pyrex dish. Sprinkle on cheese. Pour cream over this. Cover and bake at 350° for 1 hour. Uncover and bake ½ hour longer.

REFEREE'S NOTE: A staple sure to please the entire family.

GLORIFIED ASPARAGUS

2 LARGE BUNCHES ASPARAGUS

½ C. BUTTER

¼ C. FINE SOFT BREAD CRUMBS

SALT AND PEPPER

2 HARD COOKED EGGS, CHOPPED

1 TBSP. PARSLEY, FINELY CHOPPED

Cook asparagus. Melt butter, stir in bread crumbs. Cook until crumbs are brown. Salt and pepper. Arrange asparagus on hot platter. Drizzle with buttered crumbs, chopped eggs and parsley. Serves 8.

REFEREE'S NOTE: A delicacy for an elegant dinner party for eight — or two.

VINCE'S "GREENHOUSE" ZUCCHINI BREAD

3 EGGS

2 C. SUGAR

1 C. OIL

2 C. ZUCCHINI, CHOPPED

2½ C. FLOUR

2 TSP. BAKING SODA

½ TSP. BAKING POWDER

1 TSP. CINNAMON

2 TSP. VANILLA

½ C. RAISINS

½ C. NUTS, CHOPPED

by VINCE COSTELLO

(Former Cleveland Browns MLB)

Cream sugar, oil, eggs and sifted dry ingredients. Stir in zucchini, add nuts and vanilla. Stir. Bake in 2 greased and floured 9x5x3″ loaf pans for 1 hour at 325°.

NOTES FROM THE BENCH: *"This bread is served at the salad bar in our restaurant. Customers constantly rave about it. It helps make the salad bar the best in Kansas City."*

REFEREE'S NOTE: *And you thought the second trip back to the salad bar was for more salad!*

ALL-STAR PINEAPPLE AND CARROTS

1 LB. CARROTS

½ C. WATER

½ TSP. SALT

3 GREEN ONIONS

2 TSP. MARGARINE

¾ C. PINEAPPLE CHUNKS

¼ TSP. PICKLE SPICE OR DILL

SALT AND PEPPER

Cut carrots in 3″ strips ⅜″ thick. Put into a 10″ skillet with water and ½ tsp. salt. Cover and bring to boil. Lower heat and simmer until crispy tender, about 5-10 mins. Remove carrots from skillet. Trim and cut onions into thin diagonal slices. When about 7 tsp. of liquid is left in pan, add margarine and turn up heat until margarine is bubbly. Add drained pineapple, onion and dill. Heat and stir for a minute or two. Add carrots and stir. Serve immediately. Serves 6.

REFEREE'S NOTE: *An exciting vegetable dish — very out of the ordinary, very all-star, it will be eaten all up.*

Here are some "Game Plans" that might make you a star the next time you entertain. The Monday night football menu has an Italian flair. The brunch menu is a much used combination for entertaining or for special occasion breakfasts. The menu for the cold-weather tailgate has been put together to "warm" you up before the game. For a special pre-season tailgate, the menu is tailored to keep you "cool" before entering a "hot game." The special dinner menu is calculated to impress, but a word of caution, relax, and don't count calories. The "Training Table Menu" will soothe the conscience and make cutting down a pleasure.

MONDAY NIGHT FOOTBALL MENU
LASAGNA — MALAVASI

CAESAR SALAD — RON KRAMER

CHEESE BREAD — BOOZER

RASPBERRY RAINBOW CAKE — GETTY

TRAINING TABLE MENU
CRAB MEAT APPETIZERS — LICK

WEIGH-IN TORSK — REICHOW

STAUBACH'S SPINACH SALAD — STAUBACH
(or, to skim a few more calories off this menu,
substitute a plain green salad with lemon wedges)

STRAWBERRIES JULIET

BRUNCH
MORNING SMILE

HOT CURRIED FRUIT

SAUSAGE AND GRITS CASSEROLE — MINER

BANANA BREAD — KONCAR

PRE-SEASON TAILGATE AT 3 O'CLOCK
AVOCADO SOUP

VEGETABLE PLATTER WITH DILL AND
CURRY DIPS

PEPPERED BEEF SANDWICHES

RAW APPLE CAKE — CRONAN

DINNER — THE LONG BOMB, THROWING CALORIE-CAUTION TO THE WIND
ARTICHOKE ROUNDS — KRAMER

CREAM OF MUSHROOM SOUP

UNREAL VEAL — OWEN

GREEN AND GOLD CASSEROLE

ONION-PARMESAN BREAD

GRAPES A LA RASHAD — RASHAD

TAILGATE AT HIGH NOON BEFORE A CHILLY GAME
RON'S CHILI DIP — ERHARDT

WILD CARD ENCHILADAS — KONCAR

RED HOT CORN BREAD — BOLINGER

ALLEY OOP COOKIES — OWENS

CHOCOLATE BARS

MOCHA SPICED COFFEE

Tailgater's Survival Tips

The sport of tailgating, a popular midwest phenomenon, is widely becoming recognized as a perfect pre-game festivity, post-game wind-down, or both! Listed below are a few additions to your tailgating "Game Plan." They will eliminate worry about your "parking lot party." Of course, different "themes" are for you to conjure up; we've supplied some creative yet basic tailgating tips.

Wicker paper plate holders are terrific. They're re-usable, support the very least expensive plates and prevent "soggy" tailgating china.

Don't forget your cooler! It doubles as a great "sit-upon" for weary tailgaters while keeping your party on ice.

Overlooking a can or wine bottle opener can delay "uncorking" your tailgate.

A spicy tailgate should never be without salt, pepper and catsup. They do no one any good when you leave them at home.

A card table offers a lovely support for a tailgate buffet.

Some pita bread (pocket bread) affords a variety of "stuffings" only the limits of your imagination hinders.

A hot pot or thermos patiently keeps hot spiced wine or cider piping throughout the tailgate and four quarters.

Soups and stews stay steaming in a wide mouth thermos.

Trash bags are a multi-purpose item. Not only do they keep the parking lot beautiful, they're slick raincoats!

Newspaper lends itself for an unbeatable insulator when transferring hot casseroles to the game.

Remember commercial wet-wipes are ideal for easy clean-ups from those sticky, finger-lickin' good goodies.

Throw in a roll of paper toweling along with your other tailgating staples. Big spills aren't a crisis with paper towels on hand.

You may not think "elegance" and "tailgating" could even be closely related, but table cloths, fresh flowers, complete bar set ups and silver pitchers have graced many tailgating festivities. Don't be shy.

Using a colorful flag or pennant from your car antenna will announce your tailgating site to wandering guests or latecomers.

Be sure your grill or hibachi is a safe distance from your car's fuel tank — we'd hate to see your party go up in smoke!

Plastic knives, forks and spoons are the only answer for outdoor fare. Save them, they're just as good re-cycled from one tailgate to the next.

If weather looks at all threatening and you're planning a big tailgating party, rent a tent and put a roof over your head!

Your spirits shouldn't slump two minutes after the two-minute warning. Celebrate or sulk with champagne and brownies or coffee and cake after the game. Skip the traffic battle and finish your last course of your tailgating "Game Plan."

WINE

**SOME GRANDSTAND TIPS FOR CREATIVE WINE COOKING
AND CASUAL WINE SIPPING**

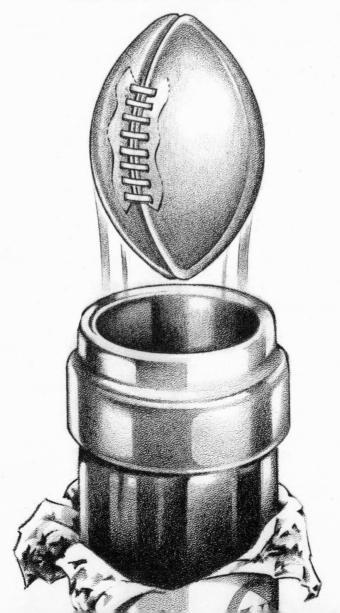

Some Grandstand Tips for Creative Wine Cooking and Casual Wine Sipping

A glass of wine to accompany your meal — a piece of chicken, a simple hamburger, a casserole or even a sandwich, turns an everyday meal into a feast. Don't wait for a special occasion or company to serve wine, always have some half bottles on hand. The inviting appearance of wine at your table to the most sophisticated sipper and even to the casual wine drinker creates a magic atmosphere and embellishes the flavor of your foods.

Use wines in cooking like you would use salt and pepper and herbs and spices — sparingly and subtly.

A wine that is not fit to drink should not be used in cooking. A good dish can be ruined by adding poor wine.

Too much wine will overpower food. A choice cut of meat can be ruined by use of too much wine while marinating or cooking. One should be able to detect the slightest hint of wine, or fine herbs, in the food.

Your table wines should be served in a large wine glass, 7 ounces in size, and filled less than half full.

Chill all white, rosé and sweet wines. Serve the red wines at room temperature.

Chill white and rosé wines only on the day you plan to serve them. Lay bottles in bottom of your refrigerator for a few hours before serving or in an ice bucket for about 45 minutes.

Wines should never be chilled in the freezer.

To avoid spoilage of jug wine, pour it into five wine bottles or screw-top soda bottles.

If jug wine seems to have gone off a bit and has a tart taste, salvage it by making sangria. Slices of lemon, orange and enough sugar to mask the tart taste will sweeten the wine to a pleasant taste — serve it over ice and add a dash of club soda for sparkle!

Metric conversions for jug wines: Half gallon is replaced by the 1.5-liter magnum (50.7 ounces) and the gallon jug is replaced by the 3-liter jeroboam (101.4 ounces).

When baking a ham, baste it with a few tablespoons of sweet Madeira for an intriguing flavor.

For a slimming alternative to a rich dessert, use a tablespoon of Amaretto over broiled grapefruit.

To give steak a spirited touch, saturate a piece of cheese-cloth in red wine. Wrap it around your steaks, cover tightly with foil and refrigerate for an hour. Before broiling, uncover and wipe dry.

To enhance the flavor of baked chicken, baste it with butter and medium-dry white wine.

For fish dishes, pat dry and sprinkle with medium-dry white wine before preparing for broiling, baking or frying.

Rosé wines are eminently agreeable and can be served with all foods.

For an inexpensive alternative, buy jug wines. If you don't have smaller bottles to keep the wine, store the partially empty jug in the refrigerator.

White wines fill the bill for fish, fowl and light meats — however, remember, whatever suits your taste is what should dictate your choice of wines.

Red wines go nicely with red meats, game and cheese.

Have you heard Chianti is classified as the "spaghetti wine"?

Half-liter wine carafes arranged at your table so that two people can share one will add to a beautiful table setting.

When wine is used in cooking, the alcohol evaporates. Only the flavor is left.

Try substituting white dinner wine or Sherry for half the liquid needed in a cake, cooky, pudding or pie filling mix for a pleasantly delicious flavor.

For extra showmanship with vegetables, cook them creamed in a smooth wine-enhanced sauce. For carrots or celery, add dry Sherry and a light dusting of nutmeg to the cream sauce. With tiny whole onions, dry Vermouth is a delicate accompaniment.

Beat Sherry-butter into cooked squash, sweet potatoes or yams for a gourmet flavor. Heat butter with a little Sherry, then combine with the hot mashed vegetable.

For a show-off savory stuffing for roast turkey or chicken, moisten with a white dinner wine, such as Rhine, Chablis or Sauterne. Follow package directions on dry stuffing. Mix, substituting wine for water. Serve the same wine with the meal to complete the play.

A good way to enliven broiled or barbecued fish is with a simple wine-butter baste. Mix equal parts butter and Rosé, Chablis or Sauterne. A squeeze of lemon or lime and a pinch of your favorite herb adds to the delicate flavor. Heat the mixture in a small pan and baste often over fish while broiling or barbecuing.

"Hot Chocolate Nasty" is one of the simplest winter wine drinks. Make instant hot chocolate in the usual manner, then add 1 tablespoon of Sherry or Muscatel to each cup.

For a new interest in chicken, barbecued, sauteed or roasted, combine Sauterne or other white dinner wine with honey, finely chopped green onion or minced garlic and a touch of soy sauce to taste. Serve the same wine at your meal and enjoy.

Turn a favorite tailgate dish — canned baked beans — into an adventure in wine cooking. To a 1 lb. 12 oz. can of baked beans, add ⅓ C. Sherry, 2 tbsp. brown sugar, 1 tsp. dry mustard and 1 tsp. instant coffee powder. The Sherry and coffee add a rich, nutty flavor that's impossible to identify, but a sheer delight to enjoy.

MICRO WAVE

A football coach would never consider substituting a quarterback for a tight end, but would use each in their most suitable position, where they can be most effective. Think of your conventional and microwave ovens in the same way. One does not take the place of the other. The microwave can be a great additional kitchen tool and save you time, effort and money.

When using one of your favorite recipes for the microwave, an easy thing to do is to find a similar recipe in your microwave instructions and check to see that the main solid ingredient is relative. For instance, if your recipe calls for one pound of meat, find a microwave recipe that also calls for one pound of meat and proceed.

With a microwave, use less liquid and go easy on seasoning as there is less evaporation in a microwave.

Use the glass or plastic cooking dishes as suggested by your microwave book and reduce the cooking time by ¼ to ⅓.

Foods to be avoided in the microwave are crisp, fried foods such as chicken, hash browns or french fries. Never try to deep fry in the oven. Candies, bar cookies, or rich cakes, for example, do well because of the high sugar and fat content.

You'll find yourself "stocking up" on such things as waxed paper, plastic wrap, glass or plastic containers and pans, a quart measuring cup and small glass cups.

The next time you forget to take the roast out of the freezer for dinner, or have to hold dinner for hours, you'll have a new appreciation for the microwave. It can "score" well for you!

Do you have left-over coffee? Keep the coffee in a jar and refrigerate until used. Pour into serving cup and heat in microwave for about 1 minute, 20 seconds.

Do you want your youngsters to fix their own egg in the morning? Teach them to take a glass custard cup, put in a little butter, break an egg, salt and pepper, cover with waxed paper and microwave for about 45 seconds. Nutritious, fast and so easy!

Is your ice cream too hard to scoop? Put it in microwave about 25 seconds, depending on size of carton.

Brown or white sugar dry and brittle? Cover and put in microwave about 20 seconds.

Plastic film sticking to your frozen meat? Put in microwave about 25 seconds.

Do you want to remove skins from peaches or tomatoes? Put in microwave about 25 seconds, let stand a few minutes and peel.

Want a quick chocolate sauce for your ice cream? Put some chocolate chips in microwave for about 2 minutes. This is a great way to melt chocolate for any of your recipes — never have to worry about drying.

Bacon pieces stuck together when you take them out of refrigerator? Put package in microwave for about 30 seconds and pieces will separate easily.

Does your family like several different vegetables? Cook them in their own plastic bags. Snip corner off to ventilate, add a little butter or seasoning, put in plastic or glass container and you have several vegetables without using more than one pan.

Do you dehydrate fruit from your garden to store for future use? Put fruit in glass pan, cover with water, cook for about 7 minutes and let stand for a few minutes. It's like fresh, stewed fruit.

Haven't got time to allow your homemade bread to raise? Do this in about 20-25 minutes by giving the dough short bursts of energy and allow it to rest in between. Consult your microwave book for exact times.

Does your child like hot cocoa in the morning? A cup of hot water in the microwave for about a minute and a half, add cocoa and marshmallows, it will make a deliciously hot drink.

Does your white sauce always get lumpy? Use a measuring cup, melt butter in microwave, add flour and milk, stir and microwave about 2½ minutes and you have a never-fail method.

Do you want a quick vegetable sauce? Add a little mustard and about a cup of shredded cheese to a white sauce for a delicious topping for vegetables or whatever.

Do your youngsters love pudding as a snack? Teach them to do it themselves in a microwave. Pour 2 cups milk into a 4 cup measuring cup, add pudding mix, stir and microwave, uncovered for about 5 minutes.

Microwave refrigerated cheese ½ to 1 minute on medium to make it easier to slice.

Remember to puncture the membrane of the egg yolk to prevent bursting when microwaving poached or shirred eggs.

Do not try to hard cook eggs in the microwave. They expand during cooking and will burst the shell.

Bottles with narrow necks may shatter if heated in the microwave.

Large food loads, like a 25-pound turkey or ham or a dozen potatoes cook more efficiently in your conventional oven.

If you don't have a cupcake pan suitable for the microwave, cut the tops off paper hot drink cups, leaving 1 inch sides. Line each cup with the conventional fluted paper baking cup. Arrange the cups in a ring on a flat plate.

Remember to remove all metal twist ties from bread and roll packages before heating in the microwave.

When cooking vegetables in the microwave, add salt to the water in the casserole before adding the vegetables or salt them after cooking. Salting the tops of the vegetables before microwaving will cause dried-out, darkened spots.

For a "microwave safe" test for dishes, measure 1 cup of water in a glass cup and place in the microwave on or beside the dish. Microwave on high for 1 minute. If the water becomes hot, the dish is microwave safe. If the dish heats, it should not be used in the microwave.

Soften cream cheese in your microwave for spreads or dips by removing from the foil wrapper, placing it in a glass bowl and microwave on high for ¼ or ½ minute.

For a casual meal when friends are over, (during half-time perhaps?) have each guest build their own sandwich. Let them microwave their creation, enjoying their individual "meltwich."

Try S'mores in the microwave! Top a graham cracker with ½ plain chocolate bar and crown with a large marshmallow. Microwave at high for ¼ minute, or until the marshmallow puffs. Another graham cracker over all makes for a yummy, gooey sandwich.

After microwaving vegetables or steamed food, lift the lid or plastic wrap away from yourself to avoid steam burns.

We tip our glasses, raise our salad tongs and serving spoons to offer our warmest thanks and induct these celebrated football personalities into our "National Food Lovers" Hall of Fame.

LYLE ALZADO, #77 DEFENSIVE END, CLEVELAND BROWNS

Lyle was drafted by Denver out of tiny Yankton College. He made history by boxing Muhammad Ali in 1979.

TERRY BARR, FORMER DEFENSIVE BACK, DETROIT LIONS

Terry played on the 1957 World Championship Lions team. He was also All-Pro Wide Receiver. Terry was considered an excellent all-around athlete at the University of Michigan.

BO BOLINGER, SCOUT, ST. LOUIS CARDINALS

Bo was a former great Oklahoma All-American and played several years in professional football. He has been a scout for many years and is highly respected in his field.

EMERSON BOOZER, FORMER RUNNING BACK, NEW YORK JETS

Emerson played with the Jets both before the NFL merger and after. He was the starting Halfback on their Super Bowl Championship team.

PETER BROCK, #58, CENTER, NEW ENGLAND PATRIOTS

Peter was a 1st round draft choice from Colorado University. He's a versatile player and can play any position on the offensive line.

JOHN BRODIE, SPORTSCASTER FOR NBC TELEVISION

John played for the San Francisco 49ers. He was their 1957 first round draft choice from Stanford. He played as Quarterback and holds most 49ers passing records.

BILL BROWN, FORMER FULLBACK, MINNESOTA VIKINGS

Bill was traded by Chicago to Minnesota after his rookie year and became an all-time favorite of Vikings fans. He gave 100% as a player and was an All-League Fullback. He played in several championship games and Super Bowls.

BOBBY BRYANT, #20, CORNER BACK, MINNESOTA VIKINGS

Bobby was drafted from South Carolina University in both football and baseball. Fortunately for the Vikings, he chose football. He's been a Pro Bowl player and a starter for many years. He has played in all the Super Bowl games for Minnesota.

HAROLD CARMICHAEL, #17, WIDE RECEIVER, PHILADELPHIA EAGLES

Harold is the tallest of the Wide Receivers, 6'8". He is a Pro Bowl player and also holds the NFL record for passes caught in consecutive games.

HOWARD CASSADY, FORMER HALFBACK, WIDE RECEIVER, DETROIT LIONS, PHILADELPHIA EAGLES

Howard was a 1st round draft choice by Detroit out of Ohio State in 1956. He was a Heisman Trophy winner and an All-American in 1955. He switched to Wide Receiver from Running Back and played on Detroit's last championship team in 1957.

JACK CHRISTIANSEN, ASSISTANT COACH, SEATTLE SEAHAWKS

Jack is in the Hall of Fame as a Defensive Back. He played on the championship Detroit Lions teams of the 1950's. He was also the former head coach of the San Francisco 49ers and Stanford University.

DICK CONN, #22, SAFETY, NEW ENGLAND PATRIOTS

Dick was signed as a free agent by Pittsburgh out of Georgia University. He played in both the NFL and WFL. A fine special teams player.

VINCE COSTELLO, FORMER CLEVELAND BROWNS MIDDLE LINEBACKER

Vince played as a Middle Linebacker for the Cleveland Browns from 1957 to 1966. He was on the 1964 championship team. Vince now owns "Costello's Greenhouse Restaurant" in Kansas City.

PETER CRONAN, #57, LINEBACKER, SEATTLE SEAHAWKS

Peter was the 2nd round draft choice in 1977 from Boston College.

RON ERHARDT, HEAD COACH, NEW ENGLAND PATRIOTS

Ron was the head coach at North Dakota State 1966-72. He coached his team to several championships before becoming an assistant coach at New England.

JIM FINKS, GENERAL MANAGER, CHICAGO BEARS

Jim was a former Quarterback for the Pittsburgh Steelers. He coached Notre Dame, and the Calgary Stampeders. He was also general manager for Calgary and the Minnesota Vikings.

TIM FOX, #48, SAFETY, NEW ENGLAND PATRIOTS

Tim was a 1st round draft choice from Ohio State. He started very early in his career in the Patriots' defensive backfield which is considered one of the very best backfields in the NFL.

STEVE FURNESS, #64, DEFENSIVE LINEMAN, PITTSBURGH STEELERS

Steve was drafted from Rhode Island University and quietly became one of the solid players on the great Pittsburgh defense. He doesn't receive the notoriety that some of his teammates do but he is considered one of their top players.

ROMAN GABRIEL, FORMER QUARTERBACK, LOS ANGELES RAMS AND PHILADELPHIA EAGLES

Roman was a 1st round draft choice out of North Carolina State. He played in several championship games with the Rams and is an All-League performer.

CHARLIE GETTY, #77, OFFENSIVE LINEMAN, KANSAS CITY CHIEFS

Charlie was a 2nd round draft choice from Penn State. He can play both Offensive Guard and Tackle.

ABE GIBRON, ASSISTANT HEAD COACH, TAMPA BAY

Abe has been associated with pro-football for many years. He was an All-Pro Offensive Guard and also coached for several championship teams. Abe was head coach of the Chicago Bears.

RANDY GRADISHAR, #53, LINEBACKER, DENVER BRONCOS

Randy was a 1st round draft pick from Ohio State, a college All-American and also an All-NFL selection. He's the backbone of the outstanding Denver defense.

OTTO GRAHAM, FORMER QUARTERBACK, CLEVELAND BROWNS

Otto is in the Hall of Fame. He played with the Cleveland Browns and brought championships to them in both the old All-American League and again in the NFL. Otto holds many NFL records.

BUD GRANT, HEAD COACH, MINNESOTA VIKINGS

Bud played for the Philadelphia Eagles and played and coached for many years for the Winnepeg Blue Bombers. He also played Pro-Basketball for the Minneapolis Lakers. Bud holds one of the best coaching records in the league, winning over 200 games. He is considered by Minnesota sportswriters as the athlete of the half-century.

STEVE GROGAN, #14, QUARTERBACK, NEW ENGLAND PATRIOTS

Steve was a 5th round draft choice out of Kansas State in 1975. He became a starter his rookie year and has started every game since. Steve quarterbacks one of the most effective offenses in the NFL and is "dangerous" as a runner, as well as a passer.

JOHN HANNAH, #73, OFFENSIVE GUARD, NEW ENGLAND PATRIOTS

John was a 1st-round draft pick from Alabama University, a college All-American, and now an NFL All-Pro and Pro Bowl participant. His father and brother also played in the NFL.

DON HASSELBECK, #80, TIGHT END, NEW ENGLAND PATRIOTS

Don was a 2nd round draft choice from Colorado University and was a college All-American in 1976.

MIKE HAYNES, #40, CORNER BACK, KICK RETURNER, NEW ENGLAND PATRIOTS

Mike was a 1st round draft choice out of Arizona State. He's an outstanding athlete and is a "very dangerous" punt returner. Mike is an All-Pro quality player and has been a Pro Bowl participant.

KEN HOUSTON, #27, STRONG SAFETY, WASHINGTON REDSKINS

Ken is an All-Pro player and is considered by many the premiere Strong Safety in the league. He holds the NFL record for number of touchdowns by interceptions — 9.

ANDY JOHNSON, #32, RUNNING BACK, NEW ENGLAND PATRIOTS

Andy was drafted 5th out of Georgia University in 1974. He's a very versatile player ranking high in his team's stats in rushing, receiving and kick returning.

BOB JOHNSON, FORMER CENTER, CINCINNATI BENGALS

Bob was the 1st player ever drafted by Cincinnati. They built their offensive line around him and he was an All-Pro performer.

DON JOYCE, NATIONAL SCOUT, BLESTO SCOUTING COMBINE

Don was an outstanding Defensive End with the Baltimore Colts in the 1950's. He played college ball at Tulane, played on several championship teams, and also wrestled professionally.

MIKE KELLER, ASSISTANT TO THE GENERAL MANAGER, SEATTLE SEAHAWKS

Mike is a former Linebacker with the Dallas Cowboys. He scouted for a time before becoming Assistant to the General Manager at Seattle.

JACK KEMP, FORMER QUARTERBACK, BUFFALO BILLS

Jack was the Quarterback for the Buffalo Bills during their 1960's championship years. He now serves in the United States Congress.

BILL KOLLAR, #77, DEFENSIVE LINEMAN, TAMPA BAY BUCCANEERS

Bill was a 1st round draft choice from Montana State by the Cincinnati Bengals. He was traded to Tampa Bay and is now a steady performer on their oustanding defense.

MARK KONCAR, #79, OFFENSIVE TACKLE, GREEN BAY PACKERS

Mark was a 1st round draft choice from Colorado University. He's a fine player who has been hampered by injuries.

RON KRAMER, FORMER TIGHT END, GREEN BAY PACKERS AND DETROIT LIONS

Ron was a 1st round draft choice from Michigan University. He was considered an all-time college player and was an outstanding all-around athlete. He played Tight End on the great Green Bay teams under Coach Lombardi.

TOMMY KRAMER, #9, QUARTERBACK, MINNESOTA VIKINGS

Tommy was a 1st round draft choice out of Rice University. He holds many college passing records and is now an upcoming star in the Pros.

PAT LEAHY, #5, KICKER, NEW YORK JETS

Pat signed as a free agent with the St. Louis Cardinals in 1974. He subsequently joined the New York Jets and was named to the "Sporting News" A.F.C. All-Star Team in 1978.

BILL LENKAITIS, #67, CENTER, NEW ENGLAND PATRIOTS

Bill was a 2nd round draft choice from Penn State by the San Diego Chargers in 1969. He moved to New England in 1971 and has been a fixture ever since. Bill holds a degree in dentistry from Tennessee University.

DENNIS LICK, #70, OFFENSIVE TACKLE, CHICAGO BEARS

Dennis was a 1st round draft choice out of Wisconsin University. He has been a starter since his 1st year.

RAY MALAVASI, HEAD COACH, LOS ANGELES RAMS

Ray is a longtime coach in both college and professional football. He ultimately became the Ram's head coach, and has finished 1st in his division the past two years, as well as taking his team to Super Bowl XIV.

BOB McKAY, #66, TACKLE, NEW ENGLAND PATRIOTS

Bob is a former 1st round draft choice out of Texas University. He's a longtime performer who also played with Cleveland.

RED MILLER, HEAD COACH, DENVER BRONCOS

Red is a highly successful coach who produced the first Super Bowl and championship teams for Denver. He's been in the league since 1960 after several years as a high school and college coach. Red graduated from Western Illinois University.

TOM MINER, SCOUT, CLEVELAND BROWNS

Tom is a former player and a long time scout for both the Cleveland Browns and the San Diego Chargers.

RON MIX, FORMER OFFENSIVE TACKLE, SAN DIEGO CHARGERS

Ron was a 1st round draft choice from USC and became a Hall of Fame player. A great All-Pro, who later served as general manager for San Diego, Ron is currently an attorney in San Diego.

CRAIG MORTON, #7, QUARTERBACK, DENVER BRONCOS

Craig was a 1st round draft choice from California University by the Dallas Cowboys. He was AFC Player of the Year in 1977, the same year he took Denver to the Super Bowl for their only appearance. Craig's a college All-American and holds several passing records.

STEVE NELSON, #57, LINEBACKER, NEW ENGLAND PATRIOTS

Steve was drafted in the 2nd round out of North Dakota State, the same year his college coach, Ron Erhardt, joined the Pats. He's a very aggressive player and leads his team's outstanding defense.

ARMAND NICCOLAI, FORMER KICKER, PITTSBURGH PIRATES

Armand played pro football in the 1930's with the Pittsburgh Pirates. He gained notoriety as a Kicker but he also played several other positions, including Offensive Tackle and Defensive End.

DICK NOLAN, HEAD COACH, NEW ORLEANS SAINTS

Dick is a highly successful coach of the improving Saints. He has been in the NFL since 1954 as a player, assistant coach and head coach. Dick has played and coached in several championship games.

JOHN OWEN, SPORTS EDITOR, SEATTLE POST-INTELLIGENCER

John writes six sports columns per week. He also stars as the author of two cookbooks that are compiled from his very successful food column.

R.C. OWENS, FORMER WIDE RECEIVER, SAN FRANCISCO 49ERS, BALTIMORE COLTS

R.C. was an outstanding Wide Receiver for the 49ers in the late 50's when they had a highly explosive offensive team. He was the originator of the famed "Alley Oop" pass and also became the first player to play out his option and join another team, Baltimore.

GEORGE PERNICANO, PART OWNER, SAN DIEGO CHARGERS

George owns the famed San Diego restaurant Casa di Baffi (translates from Italian to "House of the Moustache"). It was named for George's famous 15″ handlebar moustache that Lloyd's of London insures.

AHMAD RASHAD, #28, WIDE RECEIVER, MINNESOTA VIKINGS

Ahmad was a 1st round draft choice from Oregon by the St. Louis Cardinals as a Halfback. Ahmad also played with Buffalo and Seattle. He is an All-Pro Performer.

JERRY REICHOW, COORDINATOR OF FOOTBALL OPERATIONS, MINNESOTA VIKINGS

Jerry played on championship teams with the Detroit Lions and the Philadelphia Eagles. He also played Wide Receiver and Tight End with the Minnesota Vikings.

LES RICHTER, MIDDLE LINEBACKER, LOS ANGELES RAMS

Les joined the Rams in 1952 as a Linebacker. He was traded by the Dallas Texans for 11 Rams players — one of the largest trades ever. Les was an All-Pro player.

ANDY RUSSELL, FORMER LINEBACKER, PITTSBURGH STEELERS

Andy was an outstanding player with the Steelers for many years. He was a team leader, an All-Pro player and a player on their first two Super Bowl teams.

HOWARD SAMPSON, #36, SAFETY, GREEN BAY PACKERS

Howard made the league the hard way, as a free agent. He played his college ball at Arkansas University.

RICH SAUL, #61, CENTER, LOS ANGELES RAMS

Rich played in the Pro-Bowl Games 1976-1979. He also played in the NFC championship games 1974, '75, '76, '78, '79 and the 1979 Super Bowl.

JOHN SMITH, #1, KICKER, NEW ENGLAND PATRIOTS

John was born, raised and educated in England. He signed as a free agent and has been the Pat's Kicker since 1973.

BART STARR, HEAD COACH, GREEN BAY PACKERS

Bart was a former Quarterback for the Green Bay Packers in their great Lombardi Days. He has been inducted into the Hall of Fame.

ROGER STAUBACH, #12, QUARTERBACK, DALLAS COWBOYS

Roger is one of the premiere Quarterbacks in football today. He's an All-Pro player who has taken his team to many championships. He holds several NFL records and has been named Player of the Year.

JAN STENERUD, #3, KICKER, KANSAS CITY CHIEFS

Jan grew up in Norway and played his college football at Montana State. He has been an All-Pro Kicker many times and played on Kansas City's Super Bowl team.

TERRY STIEVE, #68, OFFENSIVE GUARD, ST. LOUIS CARDINALS

Terry was a 6th round draft choice by New Orleans out of Wisconsin University. He was traded to St. Louis in 1978 and now starts on that fine offensive unit.

FRAN TARKENTON, SPORTSCASTER, ABC TELEVISION

Fran brought movement to the Quarterback position. He played many years with both the Minnesota Vikings and the New York Giants. Fran holds many NFL passing records and is an All-Pro Performer who is certain to be inducted into the Hall of Fame.

JOHN THOMPSON, GENERAL MANAGER, SEATTLE SEAHAWKS

John began his football career as the Public Relations Director for the University of Washington. He entered pro football with the Minnesota Vikings and seved as the Assistant General Manager. He worked in the NFL office and was instrumental in the development of the player-management labor contract.

BRAD VAN PELT, #10, LINEBACKER, NEW YORK GIANTS

Brad was drafted in the 2nd round by the Giants out of Michigan State. He has reached All-Pro status and has played in the last four Pro-Bowl games. Brad was a great all-around athlete at Michigan State, achieving All-American in football.

STAN WEST, SCOUT, ST. LOUIS CARDINALS

Stan was an excellent Linebacker/Nose Guard with the Rams in the early 50's. He played at Oklahoma and was an assistant coach at Minnesota before becoming a scout.

JOHN ZOOK, #60, DEFENSIVE END, ST. LOUIS CARDINALS

John was drafted 4th out of Kansas University by the Los Angeles Rams in 1969. He was involved in several trades and has been a quality player for many years.

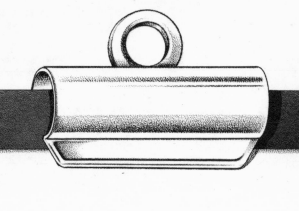

THE ROSTER

Answer to trivia questions.

Page 2 — Howard "Hopalong" Cassady
Page 5 — Ron Kramer
Page 6 — Otto Graham
Page 7 — Bud Grant
Page 8 — Roger Staubach
Page 13 — Bill "Boom Boom" Brown
Page 18 — Emerson Boozer

Page 20 — Lyle Alzado
Page 30 — R.C. Owens, San Francisco 49ers
Page 67 — Detroit's Pontiac Silverdome, capacity 80,638
Page 74 — Fran Tarkenton
Page 83 — Super Bowl XIV — over 103,000 people attended.